Modern Dramatists
Series Editors: *Bruce King and Adele King*

Published titles

continued –

continued –

Theodore Shank, *American Alternative Theatre*
James Simmons, *Sean O'Casey*
Peter Skrine, *Hauptmann, Wedekind and Schnitzler*
Ronald Speirs, *Bertolt Brecht*
David Thomas, *Henrik Ibsen*
Dennis Walder, *Athol Fugard*
Thomas Whitaker, *Tom Stoppard*
Nick Worrall, *Nikolai Gogol and Ivan Turgenev*
Katharine Worth, *Oscar Wilde*

Further titles in preparation

MACMILLAN MODERN DRAMATISTS

NEW AMERICAN DRAMATISTS 1960–1990

Second Edition

Ruby Cohn
Professor of Comparative Drama
University of California, Davis

MACMILLAN

First published 1982 as *New American Dramatists 1960–1980*
Second edition, 1991

Published by
MACMILLAN EDUCATION LTD
Houndmills, Basingstoke, Hampshire RG21 2XS
and London
Companies and representatives
throughout the world

Typeset by BP Integraphics Ltd, Bath, Avon

Printed in Hong Kong

British Library Cataloguing in Publication Data
Cohn, Ruby
New American dramatists, 1960–1990.—2nd ed.—(Macmillan
Modern dramatists)
1. Drama in English. American Writers, *1945*—critical studies
I. Title   II. Cohn, Ruby, *New American dramatists 1960–1980*.
812.5409
ISBN 0–333–53341–0 (hc)
ISBN 0–333–53342–9 (pbk)

Contents

List of Plates

Editors' Preface

The *Modern Dramatists* is an international series of intro-
ductions to major and significant nineteenth- and twen-
tieth-century dramatists, movements and new forms of
drama in Europe, Great Britain, America and new nations
such as Nigeria and Trinidad. Besides new studies of great
and influential dramatists of the past, the series includes
volumes on contemporary authors, recent trends in the
theatre and on many dramatists, such as writers of farce,
who have created theatre 'classics' while being neglected
by literary criticism. The volumes in the series devoted
to individual dramatists include a biography, a survey of
the plays, and detailed analysis of the most significant
plays, along with discussion, where relevant, of the political, social, historical and theatrical context. The authors
of the volumes, who are involved with theatre as playwrights, directors, actors, teachers and critics, are concerned with the plays as theatre and discuss such matters
as performance, character interpretation and staging,
along with themes and contexts.

Editors' Preface

Modern Dramatists are written for people interested in modern theatre who prefer concise, intelligent studies of drama and dramatists, without jargon and an excess of footnotes.

BRUCE KING
ADELE KING

To Bill Coco, who digs deeper,
and with profound gratitude for the vivid theatre of
Herbert Blau
Joseph Chaikin
Joseph Dunn

1
Looking Forward

Lean, blue-jeaned, shaggy-haired, they saunter toward unmarked seats – folding chairs or backless risers. Here and there an issue of *The Village Voice* bristles out of a jacket pocket, but no one scans the headlines; Vietnam is bombed again, blacks are arrested again, drugs are discovered again. The light discourages reading, but it is adequate for locating seats near friends, with a view of the uncurtained playing area. The programme is a mimeographed list of credits on cheap coloured paper, easily crumpled to the floor. The same cement floor leads to the playing area, on which are arranged – or disarranged – vaguely oval shapes of diverse colours. Desultorily, one by one, actors in leotards approach the ovals, depositing objects behind them. Independently, each actor stretches, twists, gyrates, apparently oblivious of the audience that gradually spreads through the seats. When electronic music sounds faintly, the actors co-ordinate into an arc to perform movements of Tai Chi Chuan. After the closing ceremonial bow, the actors take makeshift costumes from behind the ovals – that's what they were carrying – and put them on. In a procession around the audience, they clap, stamp, whistle, slap their bodies rhythmically. When they have circled back to the playing area, the house lights dim, and the performance begins.

Almost any performance Off-Off-Broadway in the mid-1960s might begin in this way. At the same time, however, professional and amateur actors were presenting plays traditionally in newly built theatres throughout the United States – proscenium, round, or thrust stage, with comfortable seats fixed firmly to carpeted floors. In the mild weather of California, or on balmier days elsewhere, other performances took place in parks or on streets. In this country without much theatre tradition, in this technological country with its monstrous film and television industries, there was a sudden burgeoning of live theatre in the 1960s, slowly subsiding during the 1970s, and holding stable during the 1980s.

I can only guess at the causes. Perhaps the behavioural rigidity of President Johnson's USA, Premier Brezhnev's USSR and Chairman Mao's China were indirectly responsible. Probably the stereotypical situations and characters of the entertainment industries inspired a widespread reaction against them. From abroad blew fresh theatre breezes murmuring of Artaud and Grotowski, both of whom were rumoured to move performance away from texts and towards the actors, away from developing plots in time and towards filling scenic space. Already in the 1950s the formal dramas of Beckett, Ionesco and Adamov eroded the conception of language as a means of communication. During the 1960s empty political rhetoric further undermined the status of words. In theatre the human body began to speak more convincingly than mere words.

And yet, as soon as I hazard a generalisation about the

2

American theatre between 1960 and 1990, I realise that its opposite is also true. Happenings were far less frequent than thoroughly traditional performances. Theatre in the streets and parks was outperformed by theatre in hundreds of new buildings, especially on college campuses. 'Poor' theatres in the wake of Grotowski were countered by the most elaborate technology ever applied to performance. The fluidity of art/life boundaries was opposed by the artifice of strict style. Proliferation of theatre schools contrasted with aggressive amateurs who scorned theatre training. Entertainment-thirsty spectators on expense accounts frequented different theatres from those wooing audience participation. Traditional theatre spectators at first viewed the new theatre as a formless madness, but television soon captured snatches for home consumption. The terminology of theatre reached out to other domains – anthropology, politics, psychology, sociology; to sister arts such as dance, music and sculpture. Mixed-media experiments of the 1960s were absorbed by mixed-art experiments of the 1970s and co-opted for extravagant musicals of the 1980s. Depending on the vantage, one could view the scene as total theatre or total anarchy.

My problem in this volume, then, was selection and organisation. My approach to this problem is pedagogical; I have tried to be informative about a broad spectrum of plays. I examine only those dramatic compositions whose main driving force seems to me verbal, and I omit the mainly visual or musical (performance art on the one hand, and musical comedy on the other). Further, I limit this survey to those dramatists who have produced an available body of work, and by 'available' I mean published.

Only a small fraction survives (in print) of the plays performed in the United States during the last three decades. Hundreds of new playwrights were offered performance opportunities in the Off-Off-Broadway fervour of the 1960s and in many new regional theatres. Paradoxically, this easy access to performance was countered by the hard fact that almost no contemporary American dramatist could afford to devote full energy to playwriting. Unlike British playwrights, the Americans could not develop the subtleties of their craft by stints in film and television, because these American media tend to appeal to the lowest common denominator of response. Nevertheless, dozens of contemporary dramatists have produced a substantial body of plays expressing their deep concerns, while earning a livelihood in other ways.

American dramatists – to flash backwards briefly – have long lived in a situation of quasi-contempt. In the nineteenth century there was no redress against plagiarism; in the twentieth century copyright has rarely assured an income. By the mid-twentieth century New York City's Broadway had a stranglehold on the drama market, and, breaking away, Off-Broadway was born in the mid-1950s. Obie or Off-Broadway awards began in 1956. Downtown from New York's theatre district in the West Forties plays were produced in small theatres before small audiences. In the main these productions were revivals of drama classics or translations of those recent European plays grouped by Martin Esslin as the Theatre of the Absurd. Few American dramatists were welcomed Off-Broadway, which was traditional in the sense that a dramatist delivered a script to a director, who then cast the play for rehearsals. Although revisions might be made, the dramatist published the play soon after opening – as on Broadway.

Revolt seethed Off-Off-Broadway. Sometimes viewed as a further step off Broadway, the second 'off' actually means *against*. Off-Broadway housed low-budget, traditional performances of plays that were intellectually

4

respectable, whether classical or contemporary. Off-Off-Broadway had no tradition but a rebellious spirit. *The Off-Off-Broadway Book* of Bruce Mailman and Albert Poland cites seventeen main performance venues, of which only four are formal theatres. The impetus for Off-Off-Broadway came from strong personalities in two cafés and two churches of downtown New York – Joe Cino of Caffe Cino, Ellen Stewart of Cafe LaMama, the Reverend Al Carmines of Judson Memorial Church, and Ralph Cook of St Marks-in-the-Bowrie. These contemporary *choregi* welcomed playwrights, performers, audiences in a wide variety of energetic, inexpensive productions. A high birth rate and comparable mortality rate typified these undertakings of the 1960s, where the playwright might function as a recorder to fix improvised scenes or as an architect to structure improvised dialogue.

It would be a critical convenience if I could pigeonhole certain playwrights as typically Broadway, others as Off-Broadway, and still others as Off-Off-Broadway, each neatly circumscribed in one of my chapters. Inconveniently, however, playwrights skip or stumble across critical frontiers, so that it is only by approximation that I assign certain playwrights – Arthur Kopit, Terrence McNally, Lanford Wilson – to Broadway, and others – Ronald Ribman, David Rabe, John Guare, David Henry Hwang – to Off-Broadway, although they have been produced on Broadway. Recent women dramatists also zigzag on and off an increasingly narrower Broadway. Then my chapters veer away from both groups to more divergent dramatists: playwrights whose work was shaped by acting ensembles; those whose medium was subservient to a message; those who gave voice to the silent; those with an anchor in other arts; and finally the major dramatists, David Mamet and Sam Shepard. This organisation avoids

chaos, but it imposes omissions: Jules Feiffer's verbal car-
toons and William Gibson's dramatised biographies, which
flourished on Broadway; Jack Richardson, who helped
found Off-Broadway; Off-Off-Broadway non-survivors.
Eric Bentley, Christopher Durang, Mario Fratti, Mark
Medoff, David Starkweather and Albert Innaurato do not
quite fit my scheme. Leon Katz, Murray Mednick and
Susan Yankowitz have published too few of their fine
theatre explorations; others may have eluded my insatiable
eye.

The British critic Christopher Bigsby remarks accurately
of what I loosely label Off-Off-Broadway, 'This theatre
was actually an assault on the notion that art is an artifact
produced by a unique sensibility and open to interpretation
and evaluation in the conventional sense.' The very nature
of theatre prevents its being 'an artifact produced by a
unique sensibility', and yet such sensibility has been a for-
mative agent of many theatres of the Western world. I
admire such sensibility, and I respond to it, often with
'interpretation and evelution in the conventional sense'.

At a time when a plethora of words denounces words,
in a period when dramas are derogated as 'scripts' and
dramatists as 'scriptors', I read a large body of plays as
literature which makes sense through words, but also as
dramatic literature which resonates through mere words
beyond sense. I read these plays sympathetically and criti-
cally, commenting in a vocabulary that the playwrights may
reject. They have nevertheless been unfailingly generous
to me, and I thank them sincerely, I also thank Mark
Amitin, Bernard Earley, John Lion, Bonnie Marranca,
and Ted Shank for their help. Sarah Mahaffy and Caroline
Egar are excellent editors and friends.

I admire the courage and constancy of the dramatists
who figure in this book, even when I do not admire particu-

lar plays. Unlike some of these dramatists in the wake of Artaud, I do not believe that metaphysics is absorbed through the skin, but I do believe that wisdom can be nurtured through every perceiving sense, including 'the conventional sense'.

2
Broadway Bound: Simon, Kopit, McNally, Wilson

The title of this chapter is an obvious pun. New York's Broadway is both a physical and cultural designation, and for two centuries its drama has enticed theatre audiences who are affluent and entertainment-oriented. The theatre capital of the United States, Broadway is fed by entrepreneurs rather than subsidies, and the dramatist is putty in grasping hands. In his *Seesaw Log* William Gibson, a dramatist produced on Broadway, offers a disabused description of the playwright as Broadway commodity:

> his work acquires three species of co-workers. The first is in the realm of economics. The producer ... must be persuaded that accepting the work will not be sheerly an eleemosynary act. ... The writer here becomes part and parcel of a complex business organization formed to manufacture and sell one article of merchandise. ... When a producer buys a play it is thus spoken of as 'his' play, and not improperly. The second species is in the sphere of the secondary arts. ... When a director

or star agrees to do a play it is also spoken of as 'his' play, and not improperly. . . . What is rehearsed is thus several plays . . . everyone wants to make art, and everyone wants to make money, and each goal is confounded with the other. The third species of co-workers is encountered thus in the shape of the behemoth-bank which contains the money, and the art becomes that of shaking it out. When a spectator sits to watch a play it is never spoken of as 'his' play, but it properly should be: none of the active hands so tyrannically molds the materials as does the behemoth's passive posterior.

Audience as broad-assed behemoth is an unflattering if humorous image to which the durable giants of American drama refuse to surrender. Eugene O'Neill, that most serious playwright, launched insidious forays against American progress and optimism. At mid-century two Broadway playwrights were subversive of its habits – Tennessee Williams of its sexual practice and Arthur Miller of its social system. More recent Broadway playwrights have sometimes undermined its aesthetic patterns.

Although I use the cliché 'Broadway Bound' as a pun, its bindings were loose on the decreasing number of serious dramas performed between 1960 and 1990. Broadway of the second half of the twentieth century can absorb un-Broadway abrasions on its sunny surface. Most serious Broadway plays, to shift metaphors, sport new tailoring for old garments – family problems à la Robert Anderson, social satire à la Jules Feiffer, suffering loners à la Arthur Laurents, lovable little people à la Paddy Chayefsky or Murray Schisgal, confused adolescents à la Michael Weller, suave wasps à la A. J. Gurney Jr. Nevertheless, a few Broadway playwrights withdrew from box-office formulae, deliberately weakening story-line, character motivation and conclusive finale. Traffic began between Broadway and the avant-garde, although the two are by definition mutually exclusive. Nevertheless, the main direction remains family realism, that most illusionistic of theatre styles precisely because it announces its style so minimally.

Today's Broadway playwright, like yesterday's, rarely springs fully formed from some Olympian thigh. Eugene O'Neill was first staged in Provincetown and Arthur Miller at the University of Michigan; Tennessee Williams wrote plays for the St Louis Mummers, and Edward Albee reached Broadway by way of the 1950s phenomenon, Off-Broadway. However, they never had the unparalleled production opportunities of Off-Off-Broadway in the mid-1960s.

Neil Simon, Broadway's most successful playwright, neither knew nor needed these opportunities. A television veteran when he turned to drama, Neil Simon might be viewed as a model of Broadway superficiality – stale situations predictably theatricalised within conventional social norms. Although his plays do take that mould, they are not mere computer products. His plays do not melodramatically present a familiar problem to be resolved by the final curtain. Full of one-line quips, his plays expose endemic predicaments rather than soluble puzzles – mismatched couples, misunderstanding generations, rival siblings, bad neighbours, and frail friends. Economically comfortable, his characters are more or less well-meaning blunderers on dead-end roads. 'I like to write about people trapped', Simon has acknowledged, and it is not quite clear whether the traps are manmade or natural, but it is clear that they clamp their victims in hilarious positions. Like the characters of Paddy Chayefsky and Murray Schisgal, and harking back to Clifford Odets, Simon's little people – often

Jewish – yearn to be a little bigger or to reach a little further. But Simon's little people are much funnier than their predecessors and have therefore been more profitable to their creator.

Born on 4 July 1927, Neil Simon exemplifies one pattern of Broadway success story – through winning affectionate laughter at familiar characters. A member of New York City's Jewish middle class, Simon is a university graduate who quickly found his niche in industry – the entertainment industry. Young enough to escape service in the Second World War, too old for action in Korea or Vietnam, Simon draws upon the escapist experience of America's urban society. His plays ignore not only wars but also racial violence, drug abuse, energy depletion. Unlike the sourly brilliant Mort Sahl or Dick Gregory, Simon in the 1950s reeled off bland jokes for comedians Sid Caesar, Phil Foster, Jackie Gleason, Jerry Lester, Phil Silvers. When Simon tried drama, his first plots were threads for a string of one-liners indiscriminately delivered by his characters. Yet Simon himself declared, 'The playwright has obligations to fulfill, such as exposition and character building.'

Simon's declaration was a dramatic anachronism by the post-Absurdist 1960s, and he performed his obligation by dissolving his plots into the situations of his central characters. Not until his fourth play did he hit on the title *The Odd Couple*, but it also fits plays written earlier and later in his career. In Simon's *Barefoot in the Park* (1963) Paul, a conservative young businessman, is the mismatched husband of Corie, who indulged in such Bohemian gestures as walking barefoot in the park. By the final curtain there is compromise; each promises to dip into the other's predilections. In *The Odd Couple* (1965), however, the couple remain at odds. Two men of opposite temperaments, rejected by their respective wives, cannot dovetail in a

11

common household, and sloppy Oscar ejects orderly Felix from his apartment. *Last of the Red Hot Lovers* (1969) returns to the accommodation of marriage – after Barney Cashman has figured in odd couples with each of the three women he attempts vainly to seduce. In *The Gingerbread Lady* (1970) the lady of the title, alcoholic Evy Meara, figures in odd couples with her homosexual actor friend, her determinedly ageless girl friend, her brutal lover, and, most importantly, her protective seventeen-year-old daughter.

The very title *The Prisoner of Second Avenue* (1972) points to entrapment, and the prisoner's wife describes their expensive cell: 'You live like some kind of a caged animal in a Second Avenue zoo that's too hot in one room, too cold in another, over-charged for a growth on the side of the building they call a terrace that can't support a cactus plant, let alone two human beings.' Chuckles of recognition ripple through any middle-class urban audience. *The Sunshine Boys* (1973) is an ironic title for a pair of retired comedians whose lives have turned to gall and wormwood, but the bitterness is funny. Simon's plays of the 1970s frame sitcom with a very hard edge. Moreover, these plays try to justify their jokes. Through thick and mainly thin of the 1960s, all Simon's characters jab with witty lines, but the jokes of *The Sunshine Boys* spout only from professional comedians, and the lovers of *Chapter Two* (1978) savour each other's quick repartee. At his best, Simon delineates trivial anxieties by means of jokes. Sour or aggressive, paranoid or paradoxical, the one-liners can sketch a landscape of contemporary neurosis.

The Prisoner of Second Avenue is as close as Simon comes to dramatising distress. The play opens on a middle-aged couple, Mel and Edna Edison, at 2.30 a.m., and Simon particularises the discomforts of night in a luxurious

Second Avenue apartment – noises, smells, flimsy walls, malfunctioning equipment and hostile neighbours. No wonder Mel experiences 'an anxiety attack' even before he loses his job.

By Act II his wife Edna has taken a job to maintain their Second Avenue prison, and Mel sinks more deeply into paranoia. While Edna telephones a psychiatrist, Mel hatches a scheme of revenge against his neighbours. By the last scene Edna has lost her job, and Mel declares himself cured. The Edisons converse in their habitual raucous accusatives, but, reversing an earlier scene, Mel comforts an Edna bewildered by *her* loss of job, as by waterless pipes and malfunctioning freezer. In the final tableau Mel's '*hand* [*is*] *holding his shovel, the other around Edna's shoulder, a contemporary American Gothic*'. Unlike Grant Wood's tableau of American strength, however, Simon's play ends on American neurosis. Mel's shovel will break no ground for plants; it will dump snow on another prisoner of Second Avenue.

Simon implies that America's cities are filled with prisoners. Contemporary American Gothic is consumer urban grotesque. Yet even in this darkest Simon play his Edisons can escape to the country, and other Simon characters are promised the rosier futures preferred on Broadway. This is markedly true of Simon's alliterative, quasi-autobiographical trilogy, *Brighton Beach Memoirs* (1983), *Biloxi Blues* (1985) and *Broadway Bound* (1986, no pun apparent). Simon's protagonist, a would-be writer named Eugene Morris Jerome, is about a decade older than he. Gene is first seen at age fifteen in 1937, when warclouds threaten Europe (and especially European Jews) while the American Jerome family is mired in the economic Depression. *Biloxi Blues* is set during the Second World War in Biloxi, Mississippi, where Gene undergoes basic training, sexual initiation and a first romance. The titular *Broadway Bound* is still only a promise in 1949, the year of the third play of the trilogy, in which the senior Jeromes separate, but the two Jerome brothers begin their successful career as comedy writers. Family plays with muted climaxes, Simon's forays into drama are warmly conventional. Eugene is at once the protagonist and the memorialist who occasionally addresses comments to the audience, but the device offers no new perspective on events. More dependably, Eugene's irrepressible one-liners thread through all three plays. In Biloxi, Private Eugene Jerome confesses to his first love, 'Playwrights named Eugene are usually my favourite' – perhaps because O'Neill was faithful to a tragic vision, which he never trivialised into comedy.

For over a decade Simon was produced annually on Broadway, however age may have withered him and staled his infinite stream of one-liners. In contrast is the Broadway career of another native New Yorker of Jewish background, Arthur Kopit, with fewer plays on the Great White Way. His first efforts were performed while he was still an undergraduate at Harvard University. *The Questioning of Nick* (1957) announces his major theme of American corruption. In a single realistic act Nick, a high-school basketball player, is so shrewdly questioned by the police that he confesses to having sold the game. *Sing to Me through Open Windows* (1959) is a single, vaguely expressionist act loaded with symbols. *Chamber Music* (1962) is set in an insane asylum where each woman patient imagines herself to be a celebrity.

The most substantial of Kopit's early one-acts is *The Day the Whores Came Out to Play Tennis* (1964), in which he shifts to Jewish intonations of affluent country-club members coached in English by their butler: 'I've always *assumed* that my job was to, um, help the members with their *diction*.' Boldly, and in bold colours, the whores arrive in garishly painted Rolls Royces to play tennis at the country club. Their effrontery does not stop at tennis played without underwear; they fart in unison, they beat a club member, they pelt the clubhouse with tennis balls, and they cut the telephone wires. Outraged and incommunicado, the club members retire to the club Nursery to toss cruel barbs at one another, while 'watching what we built collapse all about us'. Under the theatrical surface, Kopit is of course dramatising a wider chaos than that suffered by a country club, as he did earlier in the asylum cacophony of *Chamber Music*.

Before *Whores*, however, Kopit arrived on Broadway in 1962 (via Cambridge, Massachusetts, 1960, and London, 1961) with a title that soon became the subject of tiresome jokes – *Oh Dad, Poor Dad, Mamma's Hung You in the Closet and I'm Feelin' So Sad: A Pseudoclassical Tragifarce in a Bastard French Tradition*. Both title and subtitle are accurate; Mamma or Madame Rosepettle carries her husband's coffined corpse on her travels, and she hangs him in the closet of any hotel where she stays. This saddens her seventeen-year-old son, a stuttering, mother-dominated Oedipus. The play is farcical in such high jinks as a wooing chase, a near-seduction, a corpse falling from a closet, but a tragic note is struck in the violent death – by smothering – of the misguided Rosalie, who undertakes the hero's sexual initiation. The 'bastard French tradition' has been analysed by Martin Esslin as Theatre of the Absurd. What neither Kopit's title nor his subtitle indicates is the parodic basis of the play: not only Sophocles and the Absurd, but also Tennessee Williams, with the Venus fly-traps and piranha fish of *Suddenly Last Summer*, and the ubiquitous Rose of *The Rose Tattoo*. Dürrenmatt contributes the imperious millionairess and travelling coffin from *The Visit*. Madame Rosepettle vents her passion in melodramatic clichés or the grandiloquent rhetoric of Wilde's Lady Bracknell, but in the play's final moments she views the assorted corpsed debris and inquires, 'As a mother to a son I ask you, "*What is the meaning of this?*"' Under the parodic surface Kopit addresses that question to his audience, and the answer is easy: sick to its self-indulgent core, modern life erupts in violence.

The physical exercise of farce may have encouraged Kopit to attempt more ambitious scenography in *Indians*, which came to Broadway in 1969 by way of London and the Arena Theatre of Washington DC. The book's jacket quotes Kopit's description:

> a combination of Wild West Show, vaudeville, and circus. . . . There are dances; phony horses; things go wrong all the time – mock-murders turn into real murders, there are conversations with the dead. It's a hallucinatory mosaic; a nightmare panorama of Buffalo Bill reliving his life and trying to work out where he went wrong. The main problem is that he doesn't try very hard; he enjoys being a Wild West star.

Indians was successful on Broadway, but two discerning critics differ radically on its quality. John Lahr: '*Indians* is not a protest play, but a process play. With its uniquely American energy, it is both elusive and delightfully specific, a spectacle as well as a haunting vision. . . . *Indians* tackles the gigantic themes of American history and channels them into art.' Elizabeth Hardwick: 'To bring death and vaudeville together we would need a dramatic talent of the highest order. . . . But in this play, with its electronic buffalo stampedes, its restlessly shifting, undeveloped episodes, you feel all about you the old American attitude toward the killing of the Indians: indifference.' By quoting Hardwick last, I vote with her. *Indians* seems to me a spectacular cowboys-and-Indians melodrama updated through a role-reversal in favour of the Indians. Although faithful to his theme of American corruption as announced in *Chamber Music*, *Oh Dad* and *Whores*, Kopit does not probe below the glossy surface of that corruption.

Retreating from the public to the private realm, Kopit did not reach Broadway with *Wings* (1978), originally a radio play. An aphasic ex-aviatrix is lovingly led from a comatose state, through semantic error, to security in the relation of sound to meaning, and into a final verbal aria. (One scene recycles the idioms of *Chamber Music*, written nearly two decades earlier.) Taking command of speech as she had once taken command of her plane, the woman relives her glorious walk out on the wings of a plane in flight.

Apparently chafing at so simple a form, Kopit again reached out ambitiously, and again reached Broadway (via the Kennedy Center in Washington) with *End of the World with Symposium to Follow* (1984, revised 1987). Not as long as *Oh Dad* ..., Kopit's title is arresting as well as ironic, since no symposium can follow the end of the world – the human world which is threatened by the atomic bomb. As in *Indians*, Kopit resorts to metatheatre; his play is about a play. A mysterious millionaire, Philip Stone, offers a playwright, Michael Trent, unlimited resources to write a drama about global doom: 'Because the theater sir, alone among the arts engages, in equal measure, the emotion and the intellect. And both must be touched here, if we are to survive.' Kopit's play traces Trent's research – an investigation by his agent, Audrey (modelled on the agent Audrey Wood), the revelations of a Pentagon general, the paranoia of a hardline Russian scholar, the enthusiasm of two war-gamers in a think-tank, and the withdrawal of The Shadow. Clues do not cohere, as in an Escher drawing.

At once a mystery (why was Michael Trent chosen for this playwriting assignment?) and a satire (each character fears an atomic war but considers it inevitable), *The End of the World* ends simplistically on ubiquitous temptations of knowledge and power. In Kopit's three (moderately) different conclusions, Trent protests that he cannot write the play, and Stone retorts, 'Work on it.' Rather than inciting an audience to work on it, or indeed to participate in a symposium, Kopit's Broadway thriller titillates with familiar danger.

Two of Kopit's Broadway-bound contemporaries were not produced quite so early in their careers. In the late 1960s and during the 1970s they could fall off Broadway's tightrope into other locations than the void. Sometimes a play starts out in another place – notably the annual O'Neill Playwrights' Conference in Waterford, Connecticut, the training camp for Broadway; it is then revised toward the great white lights. Lacking Kopit's ambitious theme of American corruption, Terrence McNally and Lanford Wilson are adroit in bouncing up to Broadway, since both are eclectic in theme and style.

Born in Florida in 1939, McNally was brought up in Texas and educated at Columbia University, where he was infected with the Broadway virus. Arthur Ballet, who has encouraged new drama over the years, writes of McNally,

His career is a chronicle of recent American theatrical action – starting off with some ill-fated Broadway productions, removing them to phenomenally successful runs off-Broadway, and eventually into the mainstream

18

of collegiate and regional theatre in the United States. Finally. . .the process is reversing, and a major American dramatist is making his way back to the Big Time.

One 'ill-fated Broadway production' was . . . *and Things That Go Bump in the Night* (1962), which closed after a few performances. Mysterious night-bumps are heard towards the end of that play, but more frightening are the *words* of a sadistic family – mother Ruby, her twenty-one-year-old son Sigfrid, her thirteen-year-old daughter Lakme; her father, Grandfa, and husband, Fa, cannot hope to compete with the cruel volubility of this trio. Vicious families are not new on Broadway, from O'Neill's Mannons to Hellman's little Foxes, but McNally's family was born into an Absurdist era of obstreperous, exposition-less stage presence. The family lives underground, protected by an electric fence, but each night they offer a victim to the powers behind the night-bumps. Act I stages their preparations for a 'guest', and Act II presents him as Clarence, former schoolmate of Sigfrid. In an infernal night Clarence is seduced by Sigfrid and so humiliated by Ruby that he rushes out of the basement and electrocutes himself on the surrounding fence. The family members accuse one another of his death. While the titular bumps (a phrase from a fourteenth-century Scottish prayer) gradually accelerate, Ruby and Grandfa duel for the soul of Sigfrid. When Grandfa is defeated, he slowly climbs the stairs into the night. The guilty children freeze to the sound of Ruby's voice-over, punctuated by the approaching thumps. Cruel and elitist, the family is a remarkably intense creation for a twenty-two-year-old playwright.

McNally's Off-Broadway plays are sometimes extended anecdotes. *Next* (1967), *Tour* (1967), and *Botticelli* (1968) ricochet off the Vietnam War. Mildly political, too, is *Cuba Si!* (1968), in which an armed woman guerrilla is interviewed by a liberal reporter in New York's Central Park. In their non-meeting of minds, the guerrilla insists that the revolution is near, and the reporter insists just as didactically that America is immune to revolution: 'Cuba is for Cubans and you're a hell of a long way off base as far as anyone in the big leagues is concerned.' Another stab at a political play shares its central image with an unpolitical play: in *Witness* and *Sweet Eros* (both 1969) a human being is gagged and bound. McNally's short plays hazard broad satire, but his most extended effort in this genre is *Where Has Tommy Flowers Gone?* (1971). Tommy Flowers impersonates several artists – ballerina, musician, actor, opera singer, movie star, Marilyn Monroe, old lady, young boy, as well as teenage seducer, homosexual panhandler, and black activist. In the semblance of a plot, Tommy teams up with an old actor, Ben Delight; a dog, Arnold; and a lover, Nedda Lemon. Ben dies in a hospital ward, and Nedda is imprisoned in a House of Detention. A man from the audience shoots Tommy (in black face), and he dies with a last call to those he loved. The black Stagehand asks at the play's end as at its beginning, 'Where has Tommy Flowers gone?' He then explodes bombs that trigger a three-step extinction of lights on Tommy's photo and on the American flag. Tommy Flowers emerges as an American of cheerful, lovable anarchy, who goes the way of some flower children – to a violent death.

Blander satire marks *Whiskey* (1973), in a Pirandellian frame. Whiskey, a horse television star, is owned by the couple I. W. Harper and Tia Maria. Homosexual Johnny Walker contrasts with macho Jim Beam and sexually provocative Southern Comfort. Television actors, they are nervous and awkward when they have to appear live before the President in Houston. True to their names, they engage in all-night drinking and are trapped in a fire. Only the horse Whiskey escapes to star in a new television series, but the old troop, dressed in white and replete with wings, look fondly down at him.

Improbably, the two short plays of *Bad Habits* (1974) attained Broadway productions. In *Ravenswood* the bad habits are marital, and wealthy clients go to Ravenswood to learn to live together. In *Dunelawn* the bad habits are self-indulgent, but they are cured by reproach from a saintly doctor.

McNally's *The Ritz* (1975) is a blend of Feydeau and *The Godfather*. Set in a men's bathhouse (euphemism for a homosexual brothel), the play is an excuse for role-switching and caricature. Gaetano Proclo, married to Vivian, née Vespucci, is fingered for a 'hit' by her brother Carmine. At the Ritz, Proclo is pursued by Claude the chubby-chaser, befriended by the screaming queen Chris, mistaken for his violent brother-in-law by the soprano-voiced heterosexual detective, urged by the bath attendants to impersonate a producer for singer Googie Gomez. In spite of his girth, Proclo moves swiftly not from pillar to post but from near-orgy to near-orgy. Finally, in a Patty Andrews wig, mink coat, dark glasses and moustache, he is apprehended by his murderous brother-in-law Carmine. The genial bathhouse clients prevent carnage, and Proclo's wife insists upon a kiss of peace between her husband and brother. The play ends as a new orgy starts at the Ritz, with Carmine at its centre.

Orgies are expensive to stage, and Broadway prices continued to soar. Aside from musicals, ever more extravagant, the rare Broadway drama was compelled to frugality. McNally's *Frankie and Johnny in the Clair de Lune* (1987) is a cheap one-set two-act two-hander calculated to entertain. Johnny, a short-order cook, sees the hand of fate in his coupling with the waitress Frankie. Building on the coincidence of their musically resonant names ('Frankie and Johnny were lovers'), Johnny discovers or invents a network of coincidences upon which he wants to base a permanent union. The play begins in the dark, on the sounds of simultaneous orgasms, and it ends at dawn with Frankie and Johnny rhythmically brushing their (respective) teeth. Simmering in sexual one-liners, pathetic pasts and a lonely present, the play ends happily, in traditional Broadway fashion.

Co-opting existential anxieties, Neil Simon's characters evoke Broadway laughter. Less anxious and less coherent, Terrence McNally's characters present an unconventional surface; they may utter obscenities, shed their clothes, indulge in sexual deviation, and yet they do so with charm, and without offence. Bound to Broadway, McNally sacrificed the intensity he achieved at the age of twenty-two in *Things*.

McNally started on Broadway, fell off, but charmed his way back on. His contemporary Lanford Wilson, born in 1937, arrived in New York via Missouri and California, and the three locales provide him with play settings. In the mid-1960s he cut his dramatist's teeth Off-Off-Broadway. In 1969 he helped found the Off-Broadway Circle Repertory Company and became their main playwright, which proved a stepping-stone to Broadway.

His first plays (1964), with their treatment of unusual sexual situations, reveal Wilson's kinship with his fellow-Missourian Tennessee Williams. Most often performed is *The Madness of Lady Bright*, about an aging homosexual immured in his room among keepsakes and memories. He crosses the border into insanity with much of the bitter-sweet gentility of Williams' Blanche. A decade before

Williams' *Out Cry* Wilson wrote *Home Free* about an incestuous couple. Weak and pregnant, a wife/sister for the first time fails to respond to the fantasies of her husband/brother. Her death triggers his madness, and he cradles her corpse with the comfort that they are 'home free'.

Balm in Gilead (1965) is an ironic title, since there is no balm in the play's Gilead, a New York coffee shop peopled by junkies, prostitutes, hustlers and hoods. Wilson etches a sad little love affair in this dead end – of dope-dealer Joe and Chicago refugee Darlene. When Joe is knifed for trying to withdraw from drug-dealing, Darlene is drawn irresistibly into prostitution. Out of the depths and into the sun moves *The Sand Castle* (1965), named after a California beach house. Sad little love affairs multiply as a daughter seduces her mother's suitor, while a son is in love with the pregnant wife of a family friend who tries to seduce another family friend. Like Williams' Tom of *Glass Menagerie*, this son looks back on his past. With the exception of the expressionistic *Wandering* (1967), Wilson's short plays of the 1960s are realistic sketches of sympathetic misfits. In the tradition of Tennessee Williams, Wilson is tender to deviants, valuing them more highly than those who preserve the norms.

In the background of Wilson's plays is an 'Our Town' where sex drives are repressed, strangers are viewed with suspicion, and no one is allowed to ruffle surfaces. *The Rimers of Eldritch* (1966) dramatises the evil in the town of Eldritch, with a suspense that is rare for Wilson. Not until a late scene is it clear that a frustrated spinster has shot the town derelict in the act of rescuing a crippled young woman from a sexual assault she provoked. On the false testimony of the crippled woman and her attacker, the murderess is acquitted. The respectable members of Eldritch town, the rimers of Eldritch, close ranks to defend their frozen surface – frozen, too, in a conventional theatre mould.

With *Gingham Dog* (1969) Wilson perched briefly on Broadway. His black Gloria and white Vincent, an ordinary middle-class couple except for colour difference, agree to dissolve their marriage. Although they love one another, the 1960s drive them apart. Wilson's Gloria worries about her black identity while Vincent is a comfortable cog in a large corporation. Even on Broadway plays can end unhappily. This gingham dog and calico cat do not sleep a wink without one another, and yet they part – implicitly because each is inflexible in a racial attitude.

In *Lemon Sky* (1970) a son looks backwards, as in *The Sand Castle*. Alan relives events in a family under the lemon sky of California, which proved appealing to Broadway. Back across the country in Baltimore *HotL Baltimore* (1973) sets a group protagonist in a condemned hotel on Memorial Day: 'The theater, evanescent itself, and for all we do perhaps itself disappearing here, seems the ideal place for the presentation of the impermanence of our architecture', and of its inhabitants. Three prostitutes, one aged nineteen and two aged thirty, are in the tradition of the golden-hearted whore. Other HotL residents are an old man health freak, a spiritualist former waitress, a lesbian health freak and her frail brother. The play consists of interwoven strands of their biographies.

The Mound Builders (1975) is Wilson's own favourite among his three dozen plays, and, bold in scope, it did not reach Broadway, but it was televised. In the heartland of the United States, at the confluence of the Wabash, Cumberland, Ohio and Mississippi rivers, archaeologists unearth the mounds built by three civilisations between 600 BC and AD 700, 'piecing together shards, fragments, sherds. Clues, footnotes, artifacts, pollen grains, bones, chips.' The drama is presented through the memory of Professor August Howe (a name combining plenty with interrogation), who unearths for us the secrets, frustrations and cross-purposes of two archaeologists and their families, and of the violent owner of the mound-strewn land. As in other Wilson plays, each of the six main characters is endowed with a passion-packed biography. In contrast with other Wilson plays, however, the chaotic contemporary American culture is implicitly contrasted with that of earlier civilisations. An archaeologist and an entrepreneur are incapable of dialogue with one another; the latter flattens the mounds with a bulldozer, and both men 'vanish without trace' – the nightmare phrase for archaeologists.

With *The Fifth of July* (1978), Wilson embarked on his trilogy of plays about the Talley family – respectable, intolerant, but sprinkled with Wilson's beloved deviants. The first Talley play opens not on the fifth but the fourth of July, 1977, a symbolic year after the United States Bicentennial. The family members are Aunt Sally; her nephew Ken, whose legs were shot off in Vietnam; his sister June; and her illegitimate daughter Shirley. Visiting the Talleys is not only Ken's lover Jed but also a childhood friend, John Landis; his rock-singer wife, Gwen; and her composer. The frail plot hangs on Ken's ambivalence about selling the family estate, and John Landis's desire to 'adopt' fourteen-year-old Shirley, who realises, 'I am the last of the Talleys. And the whole family has just come to nothing at all so far.' But Wilson hints that this family in America's heartland may be pregnant with change; they will keep their land, which Ken's lover will teach them to cultivate and which will be nourished by the symbolic ashes of Aunt Sally's Jewish husband Matt.

Talley's Folly (1979) backtracks to Matt on 4 July 1944. The play recounts the courtship of Sally Talley by Matt

Friedman. Like earlier Wilson characters, Matt functions as both narrator and protagonist. Aging misfits, thirty-year-old Missouri WASP Sally strains against the family code, and forty-two-year-old Jewish Matt has no family or allegiances. *Talley's Folly* puns on the Victorian boat-house setting and Sally's final commitment to leave her family so as to share Matt's life.

The action of *Talley & Son* (1985) overlaps that of *Talley's Folly*. On 4 July 1944, the clan gathers to talk business, since an outside firm wants to buy the garment factory of Talley & Son. Old Calvin is still alive, while his twenty-year-old grandson Timmy Talley is killed in the Pacific war. Timmy nevertheless serves Wilson as narrator, un-tangling some of the devious schemes of the greedy patriarch, his philandering son Eldon, and his philandering grandson Buddy. Like Hellman's little Foxes, Wilson's Missouri Talleys batten on profit and prejudice. But each generation sports a misfit, who infuses new vigour into a family whose very name means 'sums'.

Perhaps the large cast discouraged Broadway producers of a genre they usually favour – the traditional family drama – but Wilson is deft with small casts too, and *Burn This* (1987), commissioned by the Circle Repertory Com-pány, moved on to Broadway. A sentimental love story that opens on a death and closes on a new relationship, the script is energised by 'in-character' laugh lines from Wilson's misfits – a choreographer who shares a loft with two gay men and sleeps sporadically with a screenwriter. Wilson is equally skilful in the repartee of the Manhattan art world and the back-home Missoura drawl.

Having begun Off-Off-Broadway, Lanford Wilson has steadily increased his characters' charm, making them acceptable in spite of their quirks. Both on and Off-Off-Broadway, he has been the consistent depicter of apolitical, uncommitted deviants. Unlike the stage people of his predecessor Tennessee Williams, Wilson's misfits rarely resort to violence, and they carry no mythic burden.

McNally began on Broadway, Wilson Off-Off, and yet they have negotiated similar trajectories. McNally manoeuvres his figures through the mechanics of farce, whereas Wilson allows a leisurely humour to mellow situations involving misfits, and neither peppers his plays with the machine-gun jokes that have brought fame and fortune to Neil Simon. This variety of Broadway surfaces is deceptive, for the form rarely strays from realism. Neither socially nor aesthetically do the plays threaten the loose, vaguely liberal and mainly affluent Broadway audience.

3
Roaming Around: Ribman, Rabe, Guare, Hwang

In separating 'Broadway Bound' from 'Roaming Around', I am guided toward the latter by my own impression of the playwright's compulsion. Simon alone has kept a stable footing on Broadway, whereas zigzags mark the paths of Kopit, McNally and Wilson. The dramatists of this chapter have executed comparable zigzags, and yet they seem to me further from Broadway conventions in subject and form, but not so far as deliberately to shun the white lights. Each of them has pursued his own bent – Ribman's paradoxical characters, Rabe's obscenity-marked shockers, Guare's grotesque wit, Hwang's Asians and Asian-Americans. Yet they tumbled onto Broadway in spite of self-consistency.

Ronald Ribman, born in 1932 in New York City and educated to doctoral level, perseveres in playwriting that is neither traditional nor avant-garde. Through two decades he remains relentlessly verbal and yet makes no concessions to Broadway. On the surface, he is as eclectic as Kopit, McNally or Wilson, since his plays range over medieval England, Germany in 1955, and contemporary prison and hospital. But searing them all is the theme of man's inhumanity to man. Fortunately for Ribman, Wynn Handman of the American Place Theatre, nominally Off-Off-Broadway, has a taste for verbal playwrights with serious themes.

Harry, Noon and Night (1964) follows Jewish-American Harry, a would-be artist and 'clown of failure', through scenes set in afternoon and night in Munich, 1955. In the first scene Harry pumps an American soldier for information about the military establishment, while both men mechanically fondle a prostitute. In the second scene Harry's bourgeois brother arrives in the tawdry room that Harry shares with ascetic German-Jewish Immanuel (originally played by Dustin Hoffman). The confrontation of brother and room-mate is a dialogue of the deaf, each claiming Harry for his own milieu. In the final scene Harry returns to the room at night. Even as he listens to Immanuel's account of his brother's visit, he wraps his friend in a mattress and nearly smothers him. When a German neighbour calls out for silence, Harry flings a flowerpot, evidently killing him while he damns the Germans for the Holocaust. The police take Harry away, still protesting against German fascism. Immanuel closes the play: 'What about me? Me!' That question predicts Ribman's pattern.

In *The Journey of the Fifth Horse* (1966), Ribman's free adaptation of Turgenev's *Diary of a Superfluous Man*, he skilfully counterpoints two victims. Against the original story of the spurned lover who dies lonely – a superfluous man – Ribman juxtaposes a publisher's reader who grows increasingly possessed by the diary of the dead lover. The enactment of the diary scenes in the reader's febrile imagination elicits a passionate response from the emotionally starved reader, who is rejected by two women. The fifth unnecessary and suffering horse attached to the doctor's carriage becomes a vivid dramatic metaphor for two super-fluous men, the diarist and his reader.

In Ribman's peace plea *The Ceremony of Innocence* (1967), flashbacks show the English King Ethelred resisting his family members and lords in refusing to fight their hereditary enemy, the Danes. The play traces the in-flammation toward war of even the most reasonable men of Ethelred's kingdom; his hot-headed son is killed, as is the gentle Danish princess. At the last Ethelred is alone. Provoked by the ongoing Vietnam War, *Ceremony* was televised without analogies being drawn.

The Poison Tree (1976) decried domestic war within American prisons. A white guard is killed when a black prisoner reaches through the bars and chokes him. The guard's friend Di Santis is so traumatised by the event, and by the apparent indifference of his fellow guards, that he hatches diabolical cruelties of his own. By a combi-nation of threat and bribe to a prisoner nearing release date, Di Santis has him conceal a weapon in the mattress of a prisoner about to be paroled. Discovered and charged, that prisoner hangs himself, inflaming the murderous wrath of the other prisoners. After Di Santis taunts them, the guilty victim strangles Di Santis, whom no one lifts a finger to help. As the Marxist prisoner explains, 'We are a tall black tree full of poison.' And Ribman catches the languages of several branches of that tree.

Ribman shifts tone sharply in *Cold Storage* (1977), which opened at the American Place Theatre and went on to moderate success on Broadway. The play contains a laugh a minute, but it is black laughter in a hospital conversation between two men suffering from cancer. Armenian Joseph Parmigian, in his mid-sixties, is the more acutely afflicted: 'They took out my bladder, shaved off my prostate, hooked up my large intenstine to my urinary tract, and tied my bowels to my hipbone.' Jewish Richard Landau, in his mid-forties, is to undergo exploratory surgery. Through Parmigian's relentless needling, Landau reveals that he alone of all his family escaped from Nazi Germany, when he was a child of eight. Without identity since then, he has never savoured life and can therefore accept a cancerous condition with near indifference, whereas Parmigian clings tenaciously to his residual body. Apprised of his own indifference by Parmigian's merciless insight, Landau shares a black joke with the older man, a new sense of life straining through the laughter.

I have made Landau's last laugh sound rosier than it is, for the play closes on another Ribman open question – whether the two men will sustain their courage. With Ribman's penchant for open questions and subtle reversals, it is astonishing that he arrived on Broadway at all.

Ribman's recent drama assaulting television, *Buck* (1983), found no welcome on the Great White Way. Buck Halloran, imagining how he would murder his wife and her lover, conceives of a television series of re-enacted murders. In the lust to stay ahead of competition, Buck's superiors order increased titillation in the series – explicit sex, raw violence and global coverage. They adamantly oppose Buck's attempts to humanise both murderer and victim. There is no 'bucking' their evil power.

Ribman himself has been penning television scripts that are morally far simpler than his stage plays. It is probable that *Buck* reflects his feeling about television violence, and the murder series is consistent with his theme of victimising victims. Buck is credibly and creditably in their lineage, but the victory of the wicked, life-manipulating officials is too reductive for what is at stake.

Thematic consistency also marks the work of David

Rabe and John Guare. Both have been welcomed by Joe Papp at his Public Theatre, from which he keeps a weather eye out on Broadway. Both have shifted sharply away from the subjects with which their names were linked.

Before meeting Papp, or thinking of theatre, David Rabe (born in 1940 into a middle-class Catholic family) was a university graduate who served in Vietnam. Other playwrights shook heads briefly at the Vietnam War – McNally in *Botticelli*, Wilson in *Fifth of July*, Guare in *Muzeeka* – but Rabe was actually there: 'And upon return the theater seemed lightweight, all fluff and metaphor, spangle, posture, and glitter crammed into a form as rigid as any machine geared to reproduce the shape of itself endlessly.' In reaction he bore witness to the Vietnam War in three plays.

The Basic Training of Pavlo Hummel (1971) traces a soldier's life from basic training to death in Vietnam. Flash-backs interrupt the plot's linearity, and a black surreal companion ruffles the realistic style. European name to the contrary, Pavlo Hummel is an all-American army volunteer, proud of his uniform, profanity and sexuality. Assigned to the Medical Corps in Vietnam, he has, in Rabe's words, 'romanticized the street-kid tough guy and hopes to find himself in that image'. Hummel requests a transfer to combat duty, where he is twice wounded, but he does not request the home leave to which he is entitled. Ordered again to the front, he goes to a brothel for his habitual prostitute, who is monopolised by a ser-geant. That petty officer throws a grenade at Pavlo, who catches it with his bare hands before it explodes. Tough Pavlo takes 'four days thirty-eight minutes' to die, 'and he don't say nothin' to nobody in all that time'. In Pavlo Hummel Rabe has dramatised the basic training of young American males. Only when Pavlo is dying does he reply

to the questions of surreal black Ardell with various intonations of 'Shit', in effect defecating on the macho code
by which he has lived. Hummel's military career, like that
of the good soldier Schweik, reflects sardonically on the
basic training of his country's army, but Rabe's indictment
is at once vague and limited, lacking the maniacal specifi-
city of Kenneth Brown's *Brig* a decade earlier. Pavlo
Hummel denies being a victim, animal, fool, but the play
as a whole denies his denial.

Sticks and Bones (also 1971), more sentimental and
broadly satiric, was successful on Broadway, where it won
the Tony Award over Simon's *Prisoner of Second Avenue*.
As Simon's Edisons are prisoners of Second Avenue,
Rabe's Nelsons are prisoners of their cheery middle-class
home. Easy clichés are the order of their day, an order
that is violated when Vietnam veteran David returns to
his family – blind. Lifted from a long-running television
series, the family – father Ozzie, mother Harriet, brother
Ricky – refuse to recognise David's affliction, both physical
and psychological.

Sticks and Bones wavers between broad satire of an all-
American sitcom family and the suffering of blind, mis-
understood David, who longs for the Vietnamese prostitute he keeps addressing in his fantasy. David proves to
be such a threat to his family's well-being that they urge
him to slit his wrists with his brother's razor: '*Harriet has
brought silver pans and towels with roosters on them. The
towels cover the arms of the chair and David's lap. The
pans will catch the blood. All has been neatly placed.*'

Broad satire. *Sticks and Bones* is apparently titled from
the street rhyme 'Sticks and stones can break my bones, /
But names can never harm me.' Rabe has tried to stage
the harm of contemporary sticks, stones *and* names. (The
parody of television sitcom has triggered another parody:

33

Christopher Durang's *Vietnamization of New Jersey*.)

Streamers (1976), Rabe's third army play, originated as *Knives* in 1970. Unpretentious and coherent, the play accommodates a multiple protagonist – three occupants of an army Cadre room. The title comes from the song of the paratroopers: 'Beautiful Streamer / Open for me'. Yet the original title, *Knives*, relates more explicitly to Rabe's action. At the start of the play, Martin has cut his wrist in an attempted suicide, but he is saved by his Cadre-mate Richie. At the end, homosexual Richie's enticements have resulted in the stabbing of his Cadre-mate Billy and his sergeant, Rooney.

Black Roger and educated Billy are willing soldiers; Richie flaunts his charms at Billy. Into the room come two kinds of outsiders, two drunk old sergeants soon to leave for Vietnam and rootless black Carlyle. When Carlyle commandeers the room for fornication with Richie, Billy taunts him. Anger flares, Billy insulting Carlyle's race and Carlyle insulting Billy's education. In the mêlée no one is sure of who is wounded or how seriously. When drunk Sergeant Rooney staggers in, Carlyle stabs him. After the bodies of Billy and Rooney are removed, black Roger and homosexual Richie are joined by Sergeant Cookes, ignorant of the deadly events. He tells of his own drunken evening, which has resulted in several traffic deaths; he rambles on about his pointless murder of an old Vietnamese man. In nonsense syllables, the old doomed Sergeant sings the melody of 'Beautiful Streamer' and then imitates an explosion: '*He begins with an angry, mocking energy that slowly becomes a dream, a lullaby, a farewell, a lament.*' It is a lament, too, for the destruction resulting from mindless violence. Except that Rabe's pace is never slow, the scenic description fits Rabe's whole theatre version of the American Army in the 1970s.

Only obliquely related to Vietnam, Rabe's *Orphan* (1973) reaches, beyond the surrealistic non-white figures of his first two plays, toward myth. Adapting no less a work than *The Oresteia*, Rabe intercuts it with a Manson-type family and recollections of My Lai brutality by Americans. Rabe invents a Figure who is sometimes Apollo and sometimes Calchas; a Speaker who situates the story in a cosmic context; two identically dressed Clytemnestras, ten years apart in age; a sententious Chorus. Long passages of Rabe's prose occasionally dissolve into embarrassing efforts at verse.

In the Boom Boom Room (1972, revised 1986) was greeted as a feminist play, since it explores new terrain for Rabe's persistent critique of the macho code. Its protagonist, Chrissy, is the obverse of Pavlo Hummel. As he progresses from army victim to tough guy who is an unknowing victim in an unjust war, she progresses from family victim to socially aware victim in a male-dominated society. As a dying Pavlo intones 'Shit' to all he has lived by, Chrissy wears a mask when she dances topless, hiding the gullible face that reflected her life. Father, mother, lover, gay friends of both sexes, and, finally, husband martyrise Chrissy; her very name is a Christ-derivative. Like Rabe's Hummel, Chrissy contributes to her own downfall, but her frailties are dwarfed by comparison with those of society, where the Boom Boom Room, a sexual marketplace, is Rabe's metaphor for contemporary American civilisation. It is a resonant image, but the play's language fails to render it deeply. Chrissy's lines are flat and abstract: 'people'll never be happy livin' the way I have. I mean, cruel and mean and selfish. When I didn't even have a self in me.' The *word* 'self' is an insuperable obstacle for dramatising the self.

In Rabe's plays of the 1980s – *Goose and Tomtom* and

Hurlyburly – he strives to hone a symbolic idiom for males trapped in their own cultural code. Retrieving the casual obscenities of the quasi-naturalistic earlier plays, Rabe enfolds them into the inarticulacies of two petty jewel-thieves of the underworld. At once friends and rivals, Goose and Tomtom enslave and are enslaved by their erotic partners. The resonantly named Lulu hovers over them as they sleep, and in sophisticated syntax prophesies a new meaning to love. At the last Goose and Tomtom of the child-like names contrive makeshift nests in the dark. Although they cannot see one another, they can see their respective diamonds, which become 'the light of the stars'.

Hurlyburly presents Rabe's most striking deployment of what he has called 'the poetic use of jargon' (which he hears also in the work of Mamet and Shepard). This time he blends his signature obscenities (now appreciated on Broadway) into informed reflections that nevertheless trickle into nonsense syllables, simultaneous utterance, repetition and desperately pugnacious interrogation. In a Hollywood setting, the land of the magnified image, Rabe propels his most arresting stage dialogue, which occasionally gets carried away by its own momentum.

More subtle and complex than the essentially two-character *Goose and Tomtom*, *Hurlyburly* also dramatises erotic relationships in a society without other guidelines than an antiquated macho residue. Eddie and Mickey, casting-directors, share a house, as well as liquor, dope, acquaintances and occasional women. Eddie befriends the would-be actor and ex-prisoner Phil, for whom murderous violence is the repeated response to emotional frustration. Finally Phil turns that violence against himself, and Eddie apparently learns, through his death, the possibility of tenderness. Although Rabe has been called a dark playwright, both these recent plays end on promise – a promise that has not been earned through the expletive-punctuated action. However, there is *theatrical* promise in Rabe's new control of an idiom that ranges from the hilarious to the exhilarating.

Another dramatist backing away from Broadway is John Guare. Born in New York City in 1938, given a conventional middle-class Catholic education, Guare began unconventionally at the age of ten to write plays, but none was produced until he was a graduate student at Yale University. An enlistment in the Air Force interrupted Guare's writing. While labouring over *House of Blue Leaves* (which took him five years to complete, after some ten revisions) Guare had two short plays produced Off-Off-Broadway at Caffe Cino in 1966. A year later *Muzeeka* was performed, first at the O'Neill Foundation and then at the Los Angeles Mark Taper Forum, before winning an Obie in 1968.

Muzeeka shows Guare's inventiveness and facility. Unrealistic monologues alternate with direct address to the audience as violence erupts out of domesticity. The titular Muzeeka is the canned music of conformism, which overtakes Jack Argue (whose name is an anagram of Guare). A junior executive for Muzeeka, Argue marries a nice girl, has a suburban house and a baby. On the night his baby is born, he goes to a whore in Greenwich Village for a 'Chinese basket job'. Glad to be drafted, Argue is soon in Vietnam, where the soldiers fight for television coverage of their skirmishes. When his soldier buddy offers Argue a share in his father's business and marriage to his sister, Argue stabs himself. At home his wife intones patriotic platitudes, the Greenwich Village whore intones hip platitudes, his Vietnam army buddy intones military platitudes, and a stagehand pours the ketchup of Argue's blood.

Guare in 1969 misjudged Broadway to the tune of two one-act plays, instead of the conventional one play per evening. *Cop-Out* exercises an actor and an actress in a series of roles that parody television types. The true-blue Cop (whose first baby word was 'Lease-Po') falls in love with the true-red radical. In a sub-plot super-sleuth Brett, aided by a *femme fatale*, solves a parody murder mystery. After a series of transformations that deflate American celebrities, the *femme fatale* dies in Brett's arms, and he resolves to 'get all you Commie Jewo Niggo Dago Woppo Mafio Faggo Russki'. The amorous Cop, whose vasectomy seals off his love for the hippie striker, shoots her when she insists on picketing. She lies in the aisle while the audience files out. In contrast to this parody of contemporary politics, *Home Fires* (on the same Broadway bill) is set in 1918, the night after the First World War armistice is signed. The play shows that 'home fires' are stoked by runaway servants and immigrants who deny their origin. The plays rambled to a Broadway halt within a week.

Devastated at this failure, Guare fled to Europe and returned in 1970 with *The House of Blue Leaves*, his best-known play, which had a happy run at Lincoln Center in 1986. He himself designated it as a marriage of Feydeau and Strindberg, or a painful domestic situation played as farce. The House of Blue Leaves is an insane asylum, and the inhabitants of a Queens, New York, apartment convert it into a virtual insane asylum when they scramble in and out of three doors and a window. The apartment is invaded by Artie Shaughnessy, zoo-keeper and failed songwriter, his mad wife Bananas, his culinary mistress Bunny, his AWOL son Ronnie, his movie-producer friend Billy Einhorn, *his* deaf girlfriend movie star, three nuns and a policeman. The meeting of these faithful Catholics occurs on the day the Pope visits the United States, and the sidewalks of Queens are lined with worshippers. Artie's ex-altar-boy AWOL son wishes to assassinate the Pope with a homemade bomb, but, when seized by a policeman, he tosses the bomb to the movie star. The ensuing explosion kills her and two of the three nuns. Bereft Billy makes off with Artie's mistress, and an abandoned Artie tenderly strangles his wife, marrying Feydeau of the precipitous doors to Strindberg of the restraining straitjacket.

Not only did *Blue Leaves* win an Obie and the New York Drama Critics Circle award, but his adaptation of *Two Gentlemen of Verona* (with music by Galt MacDermott) was voted the best musical. Rich and rather famous, Guare wrote *Rich and Famous* about a Broadway playwright with the farcical name of Bing Ringling. On the opening night of Bing's first produced play – but the 843rd he has written – we are flashed back through scenes that resulted in this gala event. At the play's start, Bing appears in full dress with new cuff-links initialled 'R' and 'F' for rich and famous. By the play's end, having understood the sordid seductions of Broadway, Bing takes off one cuff-link and throws it away. Bing then tries to remove the other cuff-link, but it won't come off. 'He can't give up that final cuff-link. He lowers his hands in dismay.'

Landscape of the Body (1977) parodies another aspect of New York City, but Guare sees the play as 'people fighting against the death in all our lives'. Death is grisly when a disguised detective on the Hyannisport–Nantucket ferry apprehends a woman for beheading her adolescent son. Flashbacks present the woman, Betty, arriving with her son Bert in Greenwich Village to bring her sister Rosalie back to the wholesome life of Bangor, Maine. Run over by a bicycle, Rosalie is killed, but she reappears to sing and inspire Betty who 'stays in New York to settle [her sister's] estate along with [her] hash'. While Betty works, her son Bert lures homosexuals to their apartment, where his friend Donny robs and kills them. Interrupting the promising New York careers of the down-Maine mother and her son comes Durwood Peach to lure Betty to the South. When he is committed to an asylum, Betty returns to New York, where her son Bert was robbed and beheaded by his friend Donny. In grief, Betty travels as far as her slender resources permit – to the ferry. There the detective offers Betty his love, which, after *sotto voce* advice from dead sister Rosalie, she mutely accepts, and Guare apparently believes that all's well that ends well.

Even more diffuse and self-indulgent is *Marco Polo Sings a Solo* (1977). Far from the Italian Renaissance, the play is set in Norway in 1999, where Stony McBride is making a movie about Marco Polo. Sexual and professional cross-couplings explode into intergalactic chaos. From outer space, Stony lyricises, 'I want no more solos. I crave duets. The joy of a trio. The harmony of a quartet. The totality of an orchestra. Home.' Stony is reborn as his son, but the loquacious characters nevertheless sing their solos before he returns to little old Earth.

After these sallies Off-Broadway, Guare returned briefly to Broadway with the small-cast reined fantasy but unsubdued wit of *Bosoms and Neglect* (1980). In the Prologue forty-year-old Scooper learns that his blind, eighty-three-year-old mother has cancer of the breast – in her euphemism 'bosom': 'Bosoms are fun. Bosoms are round.' Act I is a long witty duet between Scooper and beautiful Deirdre, who have for months been prowling around one another, since they go to the same psychoanalyst. Each has been suffering from neglect – Deirdre by her father and husband, Scooper in a recurrent dream. Through their respective biographies, they play witty games about neglected writers. Since they are psychologically damaged people whose psychiatrist is leaving town, they close the act violently: '*They punch each other. They stab each other. They are weeping and biting and attacking each other.*'

Act II takes place in the hospital room of Scooper's doomed mother, who nevertheless vituperatively rejects his suggestion of suicide by sleeping pills. Into the room hobbles Deirdre on crutches, and Scooper follows her into the outer world while his blind mother, unaware of his departure, confesses the event which he has been reliving in nightmares. Confession ended, she reaches for his absent hand, uttering the traditional wish of Broadway mothers: 'A better life for you.'

Admired mainly for his wit and invention, Guare turned abruptly in the 1980s to an entirely different kind of play – the Lydie Breeze tetralogy. He has described it as 'people banded together by some kind of ideals, wondering what has happened to them'. The four plays move backwards in time, *Lydie Breeze* being set in 1895, after the title character has hanged herself and her husband has killed her lover. The second play, *Gardenia*, set twenty years earlier, takes its name from a ship once owned by Lydie's father and from the flower that she cherishes but loses when her husband, Joshua Hickman, fails to water it during her absence. *Women in Water* moves back another decade to the American Civil War meeting of Lydie Breeze, a nurse, and her three wounded patients: Joshua, whom she will marry; adventurous Dan, whom he will kill; and illiterate Amos, who will become a US Senator. The four young people found a Utopian community in Nantucket – Aipotu, which proves to be a Utopia in reverse when greed, envy, and corruption corrodes their community: 'in all our dreaming we never allowed for the squalid, petty furies'. At the time of writing *Bulfinch's Mythology*, Guare's fourth play in the sequence, is not yet complete.

Although Guare has always dramatised the betrayal of ideals, the Lydie Breeze tetralogy is courageous in eschewing Guare's ready wit and grotesque zaniness. Carefully narrated in the manner of a nineteenth-century novel, the plays weave in and out of American history with a maturity that is new to Guare's theatre.

Neither Guare, Rabe nor Ribman has achieved sustained success on Broadway, and it is chance, rather than rhyme or reason, that acounts for their arrival there – Ribman and Guare with slight plays, but Rabe with such ambitious efforts that several critics have echoed Joe Papp's verdict that Rabe is 'the most important writer we've ever had'. Over the course of the last three decades, it has become fiendishly expensive to produce on Broadway, and serious plays are discouraged. Nevertheless, I close this chapter on Roaming Around – Broadway, Off-Off-Broadway and the regional theatres – with a success story that testifies to a residual unpredictability on the Great White Way.

Since the Great White Way has displayed and catered to white skins, David Henry Hwang might seem an unlikely candidate for its favours. Born in 1957 of Chinese immigrant parents, Hwang was expected to succeed his father in the family business. At Stanford University, however, he not only began to write plays but sowed the seeds of an Asian-American theatre company. Hwang directed his *FOB* at Stanford in 1979, but, developed at the O'Neill Conference, it caught the eye of Joe Papp, who produced it professionally in 1980.

Like several Hwang plays, *FOB* juxtaposes a Chinese past and an American present. The title is an abbreviation for a new Chinese immigrant – Fresh Off the Boat. Set in a Chinese restaurant in Torrance, California, the play is a three-hander involving Dale, a second-generation

Chinese-American; Grace, his first-generation cousin; and Steve, who is FOB. The two males engage in cultural rivalry for Grace, which Hwang exploits for gentle mockery of both of them. What distinguishes the play from any number of earlier new-American plays is Hwang's insertion of fantasy warrior scenes; Steve's Gwan Gung gives way to Grace's sly Fa Mu Lan, and the two young people depart to dance at a disco, with Dale tactfully removing his quasi-chaperone presence.

Similarly, in *Family Devotions* (1981, also produced by Papp) a Chinese-American family receives a visitor from mainland China. In this family, the older generation is fanatically Christian, the middle one fanatically materialistic, but the younger one seeks its own professional identity. The wise old visitor instructs his violinist great-nephew in Chinese heritage, even while demythicising the Christian family legends. Although Hwang again exploits cultural clashes for comedy, the tone is finally dark in the bright California world.

The Dance and the Railroad (1981) was developed with two Chinese actors after whom the characters are named. Set on a mountain-top at the time of the building of the transcontinental railroad, the play counterpoints two young Chinese workers of opposing temperaments. Lone is a loner, who avoids his fellow workers to practise dancing on the mountain-top; Ma is one who feels close to his comrades but is nevertheless beguiled by Lone's acting. After the Chinese labourers win a strike, the two men co-operate on a Chinese opera that celebrates their actual life, rather than a mythical hero. Finally, however, Lone remains on the mountain-top for a last lone dance, while Ma returns to his fellow workers. It is not easy to transplant Chinese culture to a brutal new country.

In *The House of Sleeping Beauties* (1987) Hwang dramatises a novelette of Yasunari Kawabata, enfolding the Japanese author's suicide into his own play. The quiet drama is distinctive in its departure from Hwang's Chinese background, and in its ceremonial language in harmony with its subject – a series of visits by old Kawabata to the titular house of sleeping beauties. Haunted by Mishima's suicide and aware of his own impotence, Kawabata finally renounces the sleeping beauties for the aged mistress of the house, who eases him gently toward death. It is a remarkably sensitive evocation of aging from a playwright not yet thirty years old.

Hwang was a minor poetic playwright until 1988, when his *M. Butterfly* opened in Washington and moved swiftly to Broadway. Triggered by a French espionage trial, *M. Butterfly* is a skilful compendium of Hwang's cultural education. Much of the play is set in China, but the protagonist is a European, thus juxtaposing a Chinese past against a European present, and the culture clash makes for occasionally comic percussion. As a student of Sam Shepard, Hwang reaches for a mythic dimension; as a student of Irene Fornès, he focuses on the telling detail, perhaps dredged from his unconscious. As in earlier Hwang plays, the narrator is also a character – perhaps a legacy of Tennessee Williams' Tom. As in earlier Hwang plays, familiar material (Puccini's opera) is subverted in a new context. As in no earlier Hwang play, however, sexual identity offers titillation, as does repeated reference to penises. As in no earlier Hwang play, he believes that he meant 'to link imperialism, racism and sexism'.

Suggested by a newspaper story, Hwang's protagonist Gallimard is carefully moulded – shy, homely, incurious, starved for power. Gallimard's twenty-year liaison with Song is fuelled by his fantasy of a contemporary Madame

Butterfly. In her own improbable explicitation, 'It's one of your favorite fantasies, isn't it? The submissive Oriental woman and the cruel white man.' In a final twist, however, Gallimard realises that *he* has been the submissive Butterfly, manipulated by a cruel and wily Oriental. Hence the title, *M.* (abbreviation of *Monsieur*) *Butterfly*. Hence, too, the success of a play that seems to defy the imperialist, racist and sexist insularity of Broadway. And yet the play titillates without disturbing: the duped protagonist is a Frenchman; Song is as much a cliché as Butterfly, and her European existence is incredible; the Chinese Communists are caricatures, and the ubiquitous lust for power is baseless. But the staging is spectacular, and the shimmering surface seems to conceal depths.

4
Ladies' Day:
Owens, Howe, Henley, Norman

For some feminists it is axiomatic that women playwrights offer new insight into the situation of women in our patriarchal society. As members of that society grow increasingly critical of male privilege, theatre doors are opening to female playwrights. But not very wide. In the main, Broadway has supported white middle-class ladies, when it has supported them at all. From Anna Cora Mowatt to Wendy Wasserstein, box office successes depict educated young ladies who reflect rather than rebel against social strictures; uncommon women behave in common fashion.

If one does not subscribe to this axiom – as I do not – why introduce a separate chapter on women playwrights? To underline the obvious – that women playwrights are as different as men from one another. Although several successful lady dramatists have graced Broadway during the twentieth century – Rachel Crothers, Susan Glaspell, Zöe Akins, and especially Lillian Hellman – they are steeped in the middle-class conventions of their time, both social and theatrical.

Only in the 1960s did female dramatists venture outside the unwritten ladies' limits. And none more boldly than Rochelle Owens, who has retreated only recently from theatre to her energetic lyrics. Born in New York City in 1936, she has worked in art galleries and publishing firms. So strong and sensual are her poems that their author was 'naturally' assumed to be a man. The stridency carries over to her drama. 'Authentic theatre', she has written, 'is always oscillating between joyousness and fiendishness.'

Owens' first play, *Futz* (1959, but revised in 1968), is the most sensational example. Farmer Cyrus Futz mates with his pig Amanda, so joyously that his townsmen find it fiendish: 'And how many tits does your wife have? Mine has twelve.' Majorie Satz reluctantly consents to a three-way orgy. When Oscar Loop and Ann Fox witness the orgy, he kills her and is condemned to hang, fulfilling the loop of his name. Accused of being 'the satan here in our village', Futz is sent to jail, where Majorie's brother stabs him. The play is an anti-Puritan parable that suited the mood of Off-Off-Broadway in the 1960s, and was subsequently filmed by the irreverent director Tom O'Horgan.

Shifting from an imaginary town to an imaginary Greenland, Owens wrote *The String Game* (1963). The play is named after a game played by gentle Eskimos during their long winter. To the disapproval of their Maltese priest, they associate their string designs with sexual fantasies. Cecil, half-Eskimo and half-German, resents the natives' indifference to his commercial ambition, and he buys the priest's support with spaghetti in rich sauce. Shocked at the priest's gluttony, Cecil slaps him on the back and causes his death by choking. The saddened Eskimos return to their erotic string game.

In *Istamboul* (1965) Owens grounds fantastic history in fantastic geography. During the Crusades, Norman warriors are lured by hirsute Byzantine women, and their wives are attracted to sensual Byzantine men. The clash of cultures mixes joy and ferocity, as St Mary of Egypt murders Norman Godfrigh. His wife Alice and Byzantine Leo make love while waiting for the invasion of the Saracens. Despite its all-embracing title *Homo* (1965), Owens' next play again dramatises a conflict of cultures – between a fantastic West and a fantastic East in the mid-nineteenth century, that time of imperialism. A quotation from Arnold Toynbee precedes the play: 'The most popular of the racial theories of western civilization is that which sets upon a pedestal the xanthotrichous, glaucopian, dolichocephalic variety of homo leucodermaticus, called by some the Nordic man, by Nietzsche "the blond beast".' We do not need the dictionary to suspect that the play will imply 'Black is beautiful .' Conversely, blond is ugly. Owens takes 'the blond beast' off its pedestal. Gelderen, a Dutch trader, accepts any humiliation to make money in the Orient, but his wife teases the workers sexually, and beautiful blonde Bernice is a cruel goddess in this mythical land of Oriental wealth.

Homo seems like a first draft of Owens' most savage culture conflict, *Beclch* (1966). The fantasy locale shifts to an African village, visited by four white adventurers. One of them, Beclch (with its hints of 'belch', 'cluck', 'kill') becomes a more monstrous goddess than Bernice in *Homo*, not only teasing men erotically, but also torturing and killing by caprice. She sickens her young lover Jose with an initiation into cock-fighting; she inveigles another lover Yago to infect himself with elephantiasis, and then to strangle himself. Her cruelties turn against her, however, since tribal law forbids her to rule without a consort. Vivid and sensual to the last, she savours her own death.

He Wants Shih (1970) again juxtaposes an exotic culture

against Western white rationality. After the assassination of his mother, the neophyte Emperor Lan is torn between her political pragmatism and Owens' synthesis of Confucianism and Buddhism. Tempted by scientific rationalism, Lan is saved from it by a kind of rebirth – not from the loins but from the head of his decapitated mother. Only then does he pursue the titular Shih, the feminine part of himself, which is an emblem for Owens' all-embracing mysterious *shur*. Lan reels from adventure to adventure – eventually imprisoned for despising the very knowledge he once sought. In the play's final scene Lan-he turns into Lan-she, ecstatically accepting rape by an army: 'Spread out my buttocks! I can be penetrated through by you, all of you!' Unlike Beclch, who is exhilarated by her own lonely death, Lan-she is exhilarated by all that is alive and passionate.

Owens' next play, *Kontraption* (1972), tempers such universal acceptance. Abdal and Hortten are, like Emperor Lan, in quest of their essential humanity. When a chemist situates it in the body, Abdal smothers him. Although Hortten permits the murder, he later regrets it. Anti-body Abdal is rewarded with a new form, a square 'with hips and ass'. When the novelty wears off, he remarks self-depreciatively: 'I am a contraption with shoes!' Only when square Abdul resorts to rape does he regain his human form. As he again undertakes to 'pierce the mystery of God', he dies – perhaps Owens' warning about those who fail to accept their human animality.

Owens' large casts, relentlessly strident language, compulsion for the actors to start 'high' – have diminished production possibilities in a theatre of diminishing spectrum, but her admirers are loyal with praise. In 1975 the avant-garde review *Margins* devoted much of an issue to eulogy of her poems and plays. Her *Karl Marx Play* (1973)

is a humanisation of Marx 'at the same time that it maintains the myth'. We see Marx assailed by family problems,
by financial worries from which Engels rescues him, and,
most inventively, by the scolding of black singer Leadbelly,
who rubs Marx's nose in his entrails: 'Marx has guts –
and he lets it all hang out.' But Marx is afflicted with 'Five
kinder, a wife and a lousy case of boils.' Upper-class wife
Jenny and perennial rebel Leadbelly fight for the possession of the soul of Karl Marx. Finally Leadbelly '*puts
a flaming torch to Marx's intestines. The others are dumb-
founded as Marx, with a surge of superhuman energy,
dashes off – to write* Das Kapital.' Paradoxically, animal
pain spurs Marx to superhuman efforts that transform life
for whole populations.

Less energetic in animalism is another Owens drama
obliquely based on history, *Emma Instigated Me* (1975).
Emma Goldman offers Owens a scope comparable to that
of Marx, but against her is juxtaposed, not the salty colour
of Leadbelly, but a Pirandellian Author. Goldman and
fictional Author quarrel about the play in progress:
'Nothing connects in this play', Goldman pedantically com-
plains. Although bifurcating into a visible character and
a Recorded Voice, the Author wants to follow her own
associative bent.

Emma's erotic entanglements alternate with her compassion for exploited women. Owens creates an ambiguous
portrait of a self-indulgent woman who nevertheless feels
pity for others; of a dogmatic woman who nevertheless
fights for freedom; of a virtual nymphomaniac who is also
an ardent feminist. That portrait of Goldman is blurred
rather than sharpened by the device of a Pirandellian
Author – a weakness also of *Who Do You Want, Peire
Vidal?* (1982).

In 1981 Owens' *Chucky's Hunch* opened Off-Broadway.

Owens reduces her palette to an epistolary monologue by a middle-aged vagrant who not only mixes Eliotic memory with desire, but sentimental nostalgia with murderous rage. Less fantastic than earlier Owens characters, Chucky scorns sympathy, but he seeks all the harder for 'someone or something necessary for the continuation of my being'. A superb actor's piece (especially as played by Kevin O'Connor), *Chucky's Hunch* at once controls and dilutes Owens' range and arresting imagery.

Rochelle Owens gives no quarter. A bold and raucous voice, she portrays vicious women that do not endear her to feminists; grotesque societies that alienate the sociologically inclined; and self-indulgent structures that offend the critics. She herself feels that her plays offer 'boundless possibilities of interpretation', but she minimises the imperatives of her work, which thrive in a free theatrical climate.

Her contemporary Tina Howe, born in New York City in 1937, might be praising Owens' work when she voices admiration of 'outrageous settings, lush language, and intense emotions' in the theatre. Howe's own plays tend to revolve around the nuclear family, although her first play, *The Nest* (1969), dramatises the discontents of three young women in the same flat.

Birth and After Birth (1973) borrows Ionescan proliferation to indict American family life. The play's action occurs on the fourth birthday of Nicky Apple (played by an adult, à la Vitrac's Victor). Husband and wife talk at cross-purposes, as in several Ionesco plays, while the spoiled child demands presence and presents. When Nicky grows uncontrollable, his parents threaten him with the cancellation of his party to which his adult childless cousins have been invited. Act II opens on that party. The childless couple are anthropologists who are far more dedicated to 'primitive' birth rites than to Nicky's birthday party. In the play's most shocking scene they describe a culture in which newborn infants are stuffed back into the womb to be reborn again and again. Both inspired and disgusted by that account, Nicky's mother takes the anthropologist through a birth that leaves her unconscious, while her husband unconcernedly rummages through his slides. Finally, the professional couple rush out to catch a plane, leaving the nuclear family to their own party: 'Four years ago today, Nicky, you made us the happiest family in the world!' Howe's satire casts doubt on that happiness.

Moving to a more innovative setting, *Museum* (1976) inaugurates Howe's preoccupation with art on stage. On exhibit in the stage museum are the works of three artists in a group show – blank white canvases of Zachery Moe whose parents are deaf and dumb; small constructions made of animal residua; and a clothes-line adorned with five life-sized cloth figures. A large cast wanders around these artefacts – would-be photographers, consumers of the recorded tour, a French couple, name-droppers, students, art enthusiasts and those who are bewildered by art, museum guides and friends of the artist, and the various guards who pride themselves on American security on the day when a madman shoots the Botticelli *Venus* full of holes. Although the satire is facile – 'What makes Williams' work of unusual contemporary relevance, however, is his attitude towards the materials he uses and the processes he employs' – it is enhanced by the visually amusing setting. Finally, Howe's museum visitors are electrified by the physical attention of Williams to his clothes-line, and they attack it for souvenirs, but the play closes on the sign-language of the mute parents of Zachery Moe, who are sensitive to the thunderous power of their painter son.

In her next play, *The Art of Dining* (1979), Howe shifts to another typical setting of contemporary Western culture: a town-house converted into a restaurant. Still rambling short of a plot, Howe enfolds a gentle satire of gourmet tastes into a juxtaposition of two women artists – the one a cook and the other a writer. Moreover, both of them practise their respective arts during the course of the play. Ellen creates dish after savoury dish, culminating in crêpes suzettes, ritualistically presented to the diners. In contrast, Elizabeth describes her mother's suffering and her own anorexia, while she manages not to taste any of Ellen's delectable dishes. Finally, however, all anxieties dissolve in Ellen's flaming dessert, which Elizabeth not only eats but for which she intones a benediction, blessing those who 'shared in the feast!'

Evidently drawing upon the same comfortable and neurotic WASP family as produced the writer Elizabeth (now fictionalised as the painter Mags), Howe won an Obie award for *Painting Churches* (1983). The title is a pun; ostensibly, a middle-aged painter works on a portrait of her parents, Fanny and Gardner Church. More subtly, the artistic activity always secretes a sacred aura. Like her predecessor Elizabeth, Mags Church suffers from the tyranny of table manners, and she too becomes anorexic before she finds a creative outlet. For the first time, however, Howe graduates from a panoramic setting to the probing of character in the Church family – the gentle senile poet, his angry and arrogant wife, and the artist daughter who finally understands their pain and her own.

Howe remains in the realm of the visual arts with her next play, *Coastal Disturbances* (1986). The protagonist, Holly Dancer, is a photographer on the brink of her first major exposition. Although she is erotically attached to the New York gallery-owner, she has a passionate summer affair with a lifeguard on the Massachusetts beach where she grew up. Interwoven with this adventure are the reactions to motherhood of Holly's two stay-at-home friends, and a final windy wedding anniversary of an elderly couple who have raised nine children. Eventually, all coastal disturbances subside.

Humorous without being witty, inventive without being startling, gradually growing absorbed in character, Tina Howe has given her own distinctive voice to women artist protagonists. Although Howe succumbs to the endemic American theme of tension within the nuclear family, she dramatises the savage and grotesque aspects of familiar scenes and intimate relationships, and she eschews pat resolutions.

The same claim cannot be made for Marsha Norman, who has enjoyed a more widespread success. However, her pat and uplifting resolutions represent a distinct departure from mainstream drama, since her plays depict the lower echelons of American society – victimised women, blacks on the margin of the law. Born in Louisville, Kentucky, in 1947, into a fundamentalist family, Norman was exposed to theatre as a child, as well as during her college years in Atlanta, Georgia. Upon graduation from college, she did social work and children's television before being offered a playwriting commission by Jon Jory of the Louisville Actors' Theatre.

Getting Out (1976) reflects Norman's work with disturbed, underprivileged adolescents; it is also her most technically adventurous play, since the protagonist splits into the submissive Arlene and the 'unpredictable and incorrigible' Arlie, played by two actresses. On the day of getting out of prison, Arlene/Arlie faces an uncertain future. Although her mother has not visited her during eight years in prison, she arrives to help clean the one-room apartment that will serve as home to the newly freed prisoner. Parental misunderstandings are inaugurated in this first Norman play – 'I ain't hateful, how come I got so many hateful kids?' The play's action traces the protagonist's rejection by her mother and her rejection of the pimp Carl, but into Arlene's present 'freedom' are enfolded scenes of violent Arlie's past. Getting out involves escape from psychological more than physical bars. Only gradually does Arlene subdue Arlie's vindictive violence. Firmly, she refuses the help of a protective but possessive ex-guard. Only when she feels confident of her own independence does Arlene accept the friendship of a female neighbour. At the last, Arlene is able to smile at a violent prank of Arlie.

Under the aegis of the Actors' Theatre of Louisville, two Norman one-acts opened in 1978 under the title *Third and Oak* – signifying the skid row of Louisville. Similar in their frail plots and extended duologues, the two plays are studies in brief bonding. The first, set in a laundromat at 3 a.m., reaches across differences of age, class and outlook to achieve a shared communion of two women. Culturally constrained to find meaning and companionship in men, Deedee is isolated by her husband's infidelities, and Alberta by her husband's death. During their preoccupation with the laundry of the absent men, each woman reveals her dependence to the other, and, although Alberta does not respond to Deedee's plea for continued communication, they have momentarily strengthened one another.

The second Norman one-act also takes place at 3 a.m., in the pool hall next to the laundromat. Of the two black men who converse, sixty-year-old Willie is the owner of the seedy establishment, and Shooter is a young disc jockey on his way home from work. In the past Willie had two friends: 'Gave the same advice, wore the same clothes, drove the same cars, drank the same beer, bout the same age, called themselves the Three Blind Mice.' But one of the friends, Shooter's father, committed suicide, and the other, the father of Shooter's wife, is dying of cancer. Willie and Shooter begin Norman's play in mutual suspicion of one another, but they close it by chalking their cues for a game of pool. Willie has revealed the power of friendship to young Shooter: '*They embrace, acknowledging at last, their desperate need, their mutual loss, and their pure lasting love for each other.*'

Nurtured at the Actors' Theatre of Louisville, Norman's plays have thrived at other regional theatres, but she gained national fame only with her Pulitzer Prize-winning *'Night Mother* (1982), which was subsequently filmed. Another conversational two-hander, the title is the understated farewell of a woman who shoots herself by the end of the play. Grounded, like all Norman's plays, in the mundane specifics of a depressing environment, *'Night Mother* rambles around the shared life of a widow and her daughter '*in her late thirties or early forties*'. Afflicted with epilepsy, abandoned by the husband she still loves, robbed by an unloving son, Jessie informs her mother of her prospective suicide: 'I'm just not having a very good time and I don't have any reason to think it'll get anything but worse.' Rather than the silent eloquence of Kroetz's *Request Concert*, wayward conversation envelops Jessie and her mother. Jessie's sense of purpose is diluted by the banality of her phrases.

Five years younger than Marsha Norman, Beth Henley (born 1952) resembles her in Southern background, grotesque humour, family focus, and women protagonists who woo audience sympathy. Studying theatre at Southern Methodist University, Henley wrote and directed her first play while still an undergraduate. *Am I Blue* (1972) is a duologue between lonely teenagers who meet by chance in New Orleans. A contemporary idiom covers a sentimentalism that recalls the immature Tennessee Williams. Henley's subsequent plays have also been compared to Eudora Welty and Flannery O'Connor, but she is neither so deep nor so dark.

Henley's first full-length play brought her fame and fortune. *Crimes of the Heart* (1978) was produced by the Actors' Theatre of Louisville, before moving to other regions, as well as New York, off and on Broadway, and then being filmed. Henley's three MaGrath sisters support each other in moments of crisis, but irritate each other in mundane matters. The so-called 'crimes' concern the sisters' relationships with men: Meg has abandoned her lover during a hurricane, Lenny of the shrunken ovary has sent her lover away, and Babs has shot her husband – all before the play begins. The action exonerates Babs, allows Meg an ecstatic if temporary reunion with her lover, and promises Lenny a longer relationship with hers. Henley ekes out her plot drop by drop while she stresses the sisters' irresistible charms.

More designedly grotesque are the characters of *The Miss Firecracker Contest* (1981). Carnelle Scott, who has a promiscuous past as Miss Hot Tomale, is determined to win the beauty contest of the title. Toward this goal she enlists the help of Popeye the seamstress; Elain, a former winner; Delmount, her cousin; and Mac Sam, a balloon-seller who enjoys almost every known disease. Although Carnelle fails to take winning position on the float, all the characters finally bask in one another's affections, and the play closes on faces aglow by the lights of the firecrackers.

Give or take a corpse or two, a comparable glow suffuses the characters of *The Wake of Jamey Foster* (1982), which opened in Hartford, Connecticut, only to fail on Broad-way. Not unexpectedly, Jamey Foster's wake is a slapdash affair, with an unmourning widow, her child-photographer sister, her dim-witted brother, his accident-prone girl-friend, and a tattooed ne'er-do-well, Brocker Slade, with a gift for inadequate responses. When the rest of the cast leave for Jamey Foster's funeral, Brocker comforts the widow with a song. The pattern of lovable, sexually active grotesques is too predictable in a drama where conven-tional behaviour is equated with villainy. Although Henley continues in fidelity to that pattern, with scattered regional productions, her most recent plays have not been pub-lished.

Bending over backwards, various (mainly male) reviewers have hailed a new feminist drama, but, since theatre has to lure affluent audiences to survive, the femin-ism is often domesticated. Owens, sometimes thought to be a male writer, fits into no convenient niche. Howe, Norman and Henley contribute more familiar (often female) characters in more familiar settings, each leavened with a distinctive brand of humour. Only minimally more adventurous than such successful earlier Broadway play-wrights as Rachel Crothers and Lillian Hellman, these women dramatists have yet to match the depth or range of such male colleagues as David Mamet, David Rabe and Sam Shepard. Only a woman critic dare make that state-ment today.

5
Actor-Activated: Gelber, Horovitz, van Itallie, Terry, Fornes

Broadway, Off-Broadway, Off-Off-Broadway are only approximations, and I have indicated crossovers. This chapter will be purer, and yet not wholly pure, in its survey of playwrights who were closely involved with performance.

In 1957 Julian Beck and Judith Malina found a home for their Living Theatre. At Fourteenth Street and Sixth Avenue in New York City, this building was not only off the Broadway theatre district in the mid-Forties; it was not a theatre at all but a former department store. Working swiftly, volunteers converted it to theatre space, seating 160. Even though the conversion broke into the minimal prose-for-photographs of *Life* magazine, this birth of Off-Off-Broadway was no signal for cigars and champagne, and baptism did not occur until 1960, by reviewer Jerry Thalmer in *The Village Voice*. The Becks opened their theatre with *The Connection* by Jack Gelber, who had carried the manuscript to them personally because he could not afford to mail it.

With the serendipity that has sustained the Becks through adversity, they chose the play that became a clarion call for the theatre of the 1960s, thriving as it did on drug indulgence, racial commingling, group improvisation, and erosion of barriers between actors and audience. Set in a makeshift room with homemade furniture, *The Connection* was staged for $900 at a time when an Off-Broadway production cost $15,000, and Broadway costs for a non-musical approached $100,000. Living Theatre actor Pierre Biner summarises their shock technique: 'Make-believe and reality were deliberately blended by Judith during intermission, when the actors mingled with the audience, asking for a fix in the characteristic tone and manner of addicts.' The daily press was outraged, one review dismissing *The Connection* as 'a farrago of dirt, small time philosophy, empty talk and extended runs of cool music'. Reviewers on quality weeklies, however, were enthusiastic, notably Robert Brustein, Henry Hewes and Kenneth Tynan. The play filled the house for some three years (not continuously), and Shirley Clarke filmed an edited version.

The jazz improvisations in *The Connection* and an illusion of verbal improvisation spurred the Becks to actual improvisation in the aleatory plays of Jackson MacLow. The Living Theatre produced only two more fully scripted plays (their twenty-eighth and twenty-ninth) – Jack Gelber's *Apple* (1961) and Kenneth Brown's *Brig* (1963). The latter, with its relentless repetition of United States Marine Corps drill, initiates the audience-assault technique associated with the Living Theatre as international wanderers. Their *hejira* was triggered by the United States Internal Revenue Department when its agents closed the Fourteenth Street building in October 1963 – for non-payment of taxes.

Before this event, the company's most gifted actor, Joe Chaikin, founded another company, the Open Theatre, to open the actor to his craft and to the audience. At first conceived as a laboratory to explore non-naturalistic (and therefore non-Method) acting, the Open Theatre worked with several playwrights during its decade of existence, notably Jean-Claude van Itallie and Megan Terry. In 1959 Joe Cino had opened his café to anyone who wanted to do theatre, and in 1961 poet Joel Oppenheimer's *Great American Desert* played at the Judson Memorial Church, directed by Living Theatre alumnus Lawrence Kornfeld.

By the end of the 1960s hundreds of pieces were performed by over a hundred new playwrights in unorthodox spaces. A minority continued to write when the swinging 1960s stiffened into the more restrictive 1970s. In a review of *The Off-Off-Broadway Book* Lanford Wilson laments how little was published by the playwrights of that effervescent decade, mentioning Julie Bovasso, Donald Dvares, Robert Heide, Corinne Jacker, H. M. Koutoukas, Roy London, Claris Nelson, David Starkweather, Arthur Williams, Jeff Weiss, Doric Wilson; four of these are published in the *Book*, as well as others unmentioned by Wilson. Despite omissions, however, a corpus of 1960s plays *has* been published in a flurry of paperback anthologies. Usually economical to stage, these plays thumb noses at the realistic illusions of Broadway and Hollywood; their authors were more or less committed to a raucous avant-garde.

The Connection was the trumpet of the Off-Off-Broadway movement, with its disaffiliation and audience infiltration. Like many of the disaffiliated of the 1960s, Gelber was a university graduate who knew his Pirandello. *The Connection* presents fictional director and author, as well as two cameramen to observe characters who are not in search of an author but who are hoping for a fix. In the first two acts the drug addicts await the arrival of Cowboy who has gone to obtain 'horse' (heroin) from 'the connection' (supplier). One of the junkies spells out the play's metaphor: 'the chlorophyll addicts, the aspirin addicts, the vitamin addicts, those people are hooked worse than me'. Gelber views us as hooked and waiting for a connection, as a decade earlier Beckett had viewed us all as waiting for Godot. Unlike Godot, Cowboy does arrive – in Gelber's Act II.

A rising action is climaxed first by the arrival of Cowboy and then by Leach's overdose of heroin (at which spectators fainted in the original production). Conventional comic relief comes from the *naïveté* of a Salvation Army sister. The play ends happily, with everyone getting his fix, and the fictional playwright remarks, 'We wouldn't all be on the stage if it didn't fit.' Fit it does, very neatly indeed, although it was considered free in 1959.

In Gelber's next play, *The Apple* (1961), he minimised plot but exploited the device of Pirandellian play, fascinated as he was by Living Theatre actors. Gelber sets on stage six actors instructed to use their actual names and not those in the text. They will improvise a show in a restaurant. In charge for the evening is Anna, an Oriental-American, with black Ace functioning like a stage manager. Gelber offers no motive for staging this show, which lacks the political and racial pressure of the ritual–ceremony in Genet's *Blacks*, playing Off-Broadway at this time. In contrast to Genet's rape/murder of white by black, Gelber's actors merely utter banal dialogue in stereotypical domestic scenes. 'No design is a grand design', announces one of the actors, but *The Apple* undermines the epigram, in spite of the many resonances of apples.

When the Living Theatre left the United States, Gelber

shifted to less radical subjects and forms – *Square in the Eye* (1965) and *The Cuban Thing* (1968). The protagonist of the former is Ed Stone, New York schoolteacher and would-be painter, who is scrappily married to Sandy. Beleaguered by Sandy's parents, envious of a painter friend, lusting for that friend's divorced wife, Ed vents his frustrations on his wife. When Sandy dies, Ed abruptly assumes responsibility, cross-examining the crass doctor and rebelling against Sandy's parents. After a few months, he marries a rich and beautiful woman, but the final scene backtracks to Sandy in the hospital, who closes the play with the vain plea, 'Don't go – Don't Ed.' He may have the painter's eye, but he has metaphorically struck Sandy square in the eye.

The Cuban Thing takes an affluent Cuban family from 1958 to 1964, and a heterogeneous collection they are – free-thinking grandmother, free-living father, avid consumer mother, revolutionary daughter, homosexual son, suave butler, two young intellectuals, as well as a CIA agent. Although Gelber views this play as 'an elaborate pun on sex and politics' which supports the Cuban revolution, its is hard to glean this from the text.

Gelber's fifth play, *Steep* (1972), opened Off-Off-Broadway at Wynn Handman's American Place Theatre. Skilfully conceived, it has not received the attention it merits. A divorced young social worker, Gil, volunteers to be a guinea pig in experiments on sleep. The experimenters are conventionally satirised by their insensitive questions, but the framework permits Gelber to plunge Gil without transition into many situations – professional, racial, erotic, fantastic. At the end of Act I Gill has achieved self-expressive freedom – apparently in a dream, and by Act II he rebels against his questioners, tries to recapture the love of his ex-wife, rejects the facile Karma of the 1960s, and almost dies. Once awake, he leaves the laboratory; the doctors predict that he will return, but it is left an open question. More subtly than in *The Connection*, more coherently than in *The Apple*, Gelber wields a central theatre image: sleep is a play-long metaphor for the way we spend our lives, our very dreams manipulated by impersonal and antisocial forces.

Gelber finds it increasingly difficult to be produced and published, but he maintains his connection with the theatre by teaching and directing. Approaching his fiftieth birthday he declared, 'Playwriting is a young man's occupation in America'. After his work with the Living Theatre, Gelber could not imagine fulfilling the demands of Broadway, and yet he could not adapt to Off-Off-Broadway by actually intruding its his scripts the improvisation that fascinated him.

Born seven years later (in 1939 in Wakefield, Massachusetts), Israel Horovitz leans in both directions to express the degeneration of modern America. I group him with 'actor-activated' playwrights not only because he studied at RADA in London, then acted and directed himself, but also because his plays were vehicles Off-Off-Broadway for actors who became famous on Broadway or in films – Diane Keaton, Marsha Mason, Al Pacino. During the 1980s, living in Gloucester, Massachusetts, he founded and wrote for the Gloucester Stage Company.

Writing plays from the age of seventeen, Horovitz has had over fifty plays produced. In 1967 he had four plays Off-Off-Broadway, which he describes amusingly in his collection *First Season*. What he does not mention is the fact that the four plays are written in four styles. In *Rats*, a parable, two gangster rats fight for a black baby in Harlem. *It's called the Sugar Plum* is broad satire with a sentimental end; an accidental death triggers competition between the victim's fellow student and his fiancée, both avid for publicity, and finally taken with one another. *The Indian Wants the Bronx* is a psychological thriller about two young toughs who torture an East Indian trying to locate his son in the Bronx. *Line*, which went on to Broadway, is an absurdist parable about five people jockeying to be first in line. After that first season, Horovitz couched his parables more realistically, particularly *The Primary English Class* (1975), in which a sexually repressed English-teacher interprets the foreign phrases of her students as dark threats.

Horovitz's most extended treatment of American guilt is dramatised in his 'Wakefield Cycle', which was written over a period of seven years, ending 1977. Taking its name from the Massachusetts town in which Horovitz was born (and which puns on the English mystery cycle), his cycle consists of seven plays, intended for five evenings: (1) *Hopscotch* and *The 75th*; (2) *Alfred the Great*; (3) *Our Father's Failing*; (4) *Alfred Dies*; (5) *Stage Directions* and *Spared*.

The opening one-acters gradually reveal acts of betrayal. In *Hopscotch* a '*thirtyish*' woman playing hopscotch is greeted by a '*thirtyish*' man returning to his home town. By the play's end we learn that he left Wakefield after impregnating the woman when they were both seventeen; intending to settle down with a new wife, he has finished playing sexual hopscotch. The characters are in their nineties in *The 75th* – a high school reunion. WASP woman and Jewish man at first fail to recognise one another, but a friendship develops through their recollections of the same childhood friends. The two players serve (1) to introduce the major theme of betrayal, and (2) to present the characters of the next three plays, which are ambitiously patterned on *The Oresteia*.

Alfred of *Alfred the Great* has made a fortune by selling

swamps in the West. He returns to his native Wakefield to seek his brother's murderer. *Our Father's Failing* reveals that Alfred Webber, like Orestes, killed his mother and her lover, but unlike Orestes he has repressed all knowledge of the deed. *Alfred Dies*, like the *Eumenides*, takes the form of a trial. Alfred's Fury-wife Emily charges him with many crimes, and on the Fourth of July she tortures him and condemns him to death. Horovitz strews his trilogy with reminders of Greek tragedy: the family name Webber recalls the pervasive web symbol of Aeschylus; Alfred's wife is his half-sister, recalling the incest in the House of Thyestes; Alfred recognises Emily's relationship to him through her hair – a scene mocked by Euripides as unrealistic; like Oedipus, Alfred seeks a criminal who proves to be himself.

In *Mourning Becomes Electra* O'Neill distanced American tragedy to a violent time – the Civil War and its aftermath – and he created in the townspeople an analogue to a Greek chorus, but within a wholly realistic tradition the events are preposterous. Moreover, Horovitz asks us to make immense leaps from the private – Alfred's childhood murder of his mother, adolescent seduction of Margaret, adult marriage to his half-sister – to the public: selling the Indians' land, marrying into a family named Lynch, profiteering on swamps.

Horovitz's last Wakefield evening moves abruptly out of the Webber plot and into experimental forms. *Stage Directions* accurately summarises the dialogue of that one-acter, in which we witness the reactions to their parents' death of a brother and two sisters. As they keep informing us: 'Richard feels responsible . . . Ruth feels anger.' Ruby feels grief and may by the play's end be a suicide. A *tour de faiblesse*, the play may also be a parable about the cultural heritage of American Jews. *Spared* is certainly an avatar of the Wandering Jew, eternally 'spared' to tell his tale, which consists of the calamities from which he is spared – in a long monologue heavily imitative of Beckett.

Horovitz has shifted style from realism to filmic violence to beast fable to absurdism – character studies in frail stories. The Wakefield plays begin in symbolic realism, move on to reach toward myth within a realistic strait-jacket, and subside into forms so experimental as to read like gimmicks. Although solicitous of his actors, Horovitz does not use their discoveries in the plays themselves.

Jean-Claude van Itallie, born in Belgium in 1936, is the playwright most often associated with the actors' work-shops of the Open Theatre. *War and Four Other Plays* (1967) are barely more than sketches; the titular war is a generational conflict between two actors. A role-reversal takes place in *The Hunter and the Bird*. Two skits parody Doris Day of films. *Where is de Queen* is a dream sequence. Beneath the parodic surface ontology may lurk, as suggested by the Doris Day titles *Almost Like Being* and *I'm Really Here*.

What brought van Itallie to public attention is the *America Hurrah* trilogy, which was not conceived as a trilogy. *Motel* (1962) predates the formation of the Open Theatre. *Interview*, originally entitled *Pavanne* (1965), depends upon their exercises. To round out a full theatre evening van Itallie quickly wrote *TV* in 1966. The three plays of *America Hurrah* stage aspects of America we are not meant to cheer. They take us on technical adventures: doll-masks and voice-over in *Motel*, choral protagonist in *Interview*, Pirandello for the mass media in *TV*.

Interview stages a chorus in a series of enactments that function through transformation technique, developed by the Open Theatre. Each actor 'transforms' without transition into a new character-type. They become priest–confessant, psychiatrist–patient, acrobatic opponents, subway riders, square dancers, and, most perniciously, rhetorical politician and silent public. At the last the actors line up '*like marching dolls*' one behind the other. They have responded mechanically to their social roles, without hint of sensitivity; that is why no one can help or be helped: 'Can you help me? Next.'

In *TV* George, Hal and Susan man a television control console, and the play juxtaposes them to the programmes they monitor. Through parallels or contrasts, van Itallie pairs the halves of his stage. At no time do the 'real' characters evince any interest in the news – largely of the Vietnam War. By the play's end the 'real' characters repeat the exact words of the television characters. On both sides of the screen we see and hear a formulaic, impervious world.

In *Interview* the actors speak in chorus and move '*like marching dolls*', but *Motel*, which has often been played alone, is acted by three actors within doll-masks, with heads three times human size. The effect is grotesque – half funny, half fearful. A Man-doll and a Woman-doll are garishly dressed but silent; an incessant voice-over is associated with a grey Motelkeeper-doll who wears mirror spectacles in which audience members glimpse their own reflection.

Emerging from behind blinding headlights, the Man-doll and the Woman-doll enter an '*anonymously modern*' motel room. The Woman-doll undresses and goes to the offstage bathroom, while the Voice, out of sync with the action, welcomes the guests: 'Modern people like modern places.' The Man-doll undresses, then inspects and strips the bed. From the bathroom come toilet fixtures pell-mell, and the Man-doll begins to dismantle the room. With rock music blaring, with the Voice enumerating a catalogue of incongruous objects – 'cats, catnip, club feet, canisters, banisters, holy books' – the couple draw and write obscenities on the walls; then they twist as though fornicating; soon they tear off the arms of the Motelkeeper-doll. Sirens and rock music drown out the Voice, while the couple behead the Motelkeeper. Headlights, cacophony, and a rush of air assault the audience. The doll couple walk down the theatre aisle and out of sight, dehumanised and dehumanising.

America Hurrah, an Off-Broadway success, derived in part from actors' exercises of the Open Theatre, founded in 1963. Membership of the ensemble changed over the years, but Joe Chaikin remained its director throughout, at some personal cost. *America Hurrah* exacerbated strains within the company, some of whom were involved with its success, others with Megan Terry in *Viet Rock*, and still others in workshops of Lee Worley or Rhea Gaisner.

With relatively inexperienced actors, Chaikin began a series of improvisational exercises based on Genesis, not intended for performance. With professional teachers in different areas – Kristin Linkletter for voice, Peter Kass for acting, Richard Peaslee for singing – the project evolved toward performance almost in spite of the actors, and van Itallie finally penned *The Serpent: A Ceremony* (1968): 'It wasn't a script that was first written and then performed. It's a script after the fact.' With this play the ensemble achieved international acclaim.

The Serpent juxtaposes the present against a biblical past in six scenes from Genesis – Creation, the Temptation of Eve (two scenes), God's curse, the murder of Abel, and 'Begatting'. Van Itallie's narrative traces a paradise lost: for example, God speaks through his creatures, Cain gradually learns to kill, modern women behave like Eve. Into these main scenes van Itallie inserts smaller acting segments through the Open Theatre technique of 'simultaneous texts', or striking juxtapositions. Thus, we see the Kennedy and King assassinations enacted and re-enacted, along with the reactions of anonymous crowd members: 'I was not involved.' Recollections of individual actors are interwoven into a mime of the ages of man. Finally, the actors sing a sentimental song and walk out through the audience. The ceremony works its way through violence to end in celebration.

After the dissolution of the Open Theatre, van Itallie relaxed with short plays and farces. *Mystery Play* (1973) is similar to but not as witty as Tom Stoppard's *Real Inspector Hound*. Both simpler and more ambitious is *A Fable* (1974). A King orders a Journeyor to kill a beast that is devastating his land. The Journeyor justifies her name, travelling to meet various figures with folkloric resonances: a Hermit, two Puppeteers, a Treebeast, a Hanging Person, a Dreamer, a Fugitive, and the Journeyor's 406-year-old grandmother. Susceptible of several interpretations, each character was developed from actors' exercises. Finally, the dangerous beast proves to be the King himself, the Journeyor turns into her own grandmother, and the Hanging Person dances jubilantly.

Continuing this penchant for simplicity, van Itallie produced what is essentially a monodrama, *Bag Lady* (1979). The familiar figure of an urban derelict carries all her belongings with her; her bags are her home. On a November evening in New York City, the bag lady, Clara, feels compelled to discard all but essentials; she therefore has a discard bag and an essentials bag. Her discourse – addressed sometimes to us, sometimes to passersby, and at deep moments to herself – springs from and returns to the miscellaneous objects in her bag.

A Russian immigrant who has learned to pretend madness in order to live independently – 'Be a good quiet crazy' – Clara orders her life. In response to debilitating thoughts she commands, 'Wipe.' Her fierce intensity rises above the trivial cares of the several passers-by. In a final image Clara sees Nazi brain seeping into the city, which will be snuffed out: 'City's over.' Against that holocaust, she must lighten her load: 'Only essentials.' Although van Itallie protests in his programme note that 'The play is not an attempt to portray the archetypal bag lady', he may well have accomplished just such a portrayal. Through illusions of grandeur that are familiar to us all, through a complex transfer of identity to Mama and doll, through clinging to commodity and yet ordering possessions into bags, through suffering turned to compassion, Clara remains an earthy lady. Like Winnie of Beckett's *Happy Days*, she is courageous in the face of catastrophe. Like the Prometheus behind both ladies, she bows to no authority. In paring her life to essentials, Clara salvages dignity when she bellows, 'Be a good quiet crazy.'

Van Itallie himself has embraced Buddhism in the quest for harmony, and two plays reflect his faith. *Naropa* (1980) is a journey through humiliation toward the privilege of discipleship. Through onstage musicians and the play of puppets dressed like the characters, van Itallie moves his protagonist toward his goal. *The Tibetan Book of the Dead* (1983) is a polyphonic visualisation of that sacred text, whose performance is hard to imagine from the printed page.

More approachable through the texts are van Itallie's works inspired by Joe Chaikin's stroke, suffered in 1984 during heart surgery. His recovery was brave, painful and confusing: he acquired full motor control of his body, but remained afflicted with aphasia. Joe's family and friends, including van Itallie, were selflessly supportive.

In *The Traveler* (1987) Daniel Moses, a world-famous composer who is almost literally torn apart by the many demands upon him, suffers heart failure even as he assures his brother by telephone, 'I'm fine.' We then view the action through the composer's mind as he 'travels' back from death's door to a born-again sense of himself. Van Itallie's text is remarkable in embedding the traveller's uncomprehending aphasia in a context that enables us to seize the total situation, where each character is an event in a voyage toward identity. The play closes in triumph: 'I am a composer. My name is Daniel' – a triumph in spite of '*some difficulty in enunciating*'.

As Daniel's profession precedes his name at the end of van Itallie's *Traveler*, Joe Chaikin practises his profession in spite of aphasia. Sam Shepard composed *The War in Heaven* for Chaikin to perform, and van Itallie contributed a companion piece, *Struck Dumb* (1988). At a time when we are only beginning to explore the dramas of the handicapped – *Children of a Lesser God* and *My Left Foot* are cases in point – *Struck Dumb* surrounds the aphasic actor with language, since words '*literally come flying at him from all sides of the stage in full view of the audience*'. Belying the title, the actor mouths these words, which he discovers on placards, plastic scrolls, television monitors and coloured pieces of paper. At once a tribute to and a play about Joe Chaikin, *Struck Dumb* is an eloquent summation of van Itallie's own drama, in its theatrical quest for human space. Like his own bag lady, van Itallie gradually pares away all but the stage essentials.

The Open Theatre brought together playwrights of different backgrounds. Jean-Claude van Itallie was born in Belgium in 1936, and Megan Terry four years earlier in Seattle. Van Itallie has written for television, whereas Terry was trained in the visual arts. She moved from designing to directing to acting to writing plays. In the mid-1950s in Seattle she staged her own plays (under a pseudonym) along with those of O'Neill, and a reviewer consigned them both to 'a burlesque house on Skid Row'. In 1956 she moved to New York, which was slightly more hospitable. Since then Terry has written over sixty plays, with some two dozen published. Since 1974 she has been associated with the Omaha Magic Theatre, and in the 1980s she was called the mother of American feminist drama.

Eight Terry plays were produced by the Open Theatre. Stemming from child's play and actor's improvisations, transformation plays broaden the actor's technical skill, since he or she has to shift sex, age, class, or even enact a lifeless object. Terry's first transformation, *Eat at Joe's*, is unpublished, but the technique is graphically illustrated in *Keep Tightly Closed in a Cool Dry Place* (1965). The title derives from instructions on foodstuff containers, but Terry implicitly commands the actor, too, to keep emotions cool while enacting the immediate situation, as in Diderot's *Paradox of the Actor*. In *Keep Tightly Closed* three men are in the same jail for murdering the wife of one of them. Without warning, they transform into General Custer's soldiers dismembering an Indian, into Captain John Smith saving two members of his expedition. Other transformations incorporate and revolve about the scene of the murder. In amassing the circumstantial evidence, Terry ingeniously portrays media caricatures – entertainers, drag queens, movie gangsters, altar boys, as well as machines. It is problematical whether, as the first directors claim, these transformations add to 'a visceral understanding of guilt', but they do provide scope for the actor to parody aspects of popular culture.

Terry has described *Comings and Goings* (1966) as 'a trampoline for actors and director'. The number of actors varies, but the individual human scenes are built around he–she exchanges; the actors also portray electric plugs, a pencil and list, signalling galaxies, and they close on a celebratory courtship scene. That same year Terry wrote her favourite play, *The Gloaming, Oh My Darling*, which is not a transformation. Two old women in a rest home share a man, or perhaps a fantasy of a man, Mr Birdsong. Temperamentally mercurial, the two bedridden women shift mood as swiftly as Terry's other characters shift roles, and Mr Birdsong intones at intervals a jingoistic view of American history. Inspired by him, Mrs Tweed and Mrs Watermellon revert to their youth, resist their nurse, and finally move into the gloaming of death.

Terry's major work with Open Theatre actors is *Viet Rock* (1966), subtitled a 'Folk War Movie'. It is a movie in its transformational 'cut' after each scene, and in the popular cultural characters at the base of the scenes. The actors assume a dozen different roles during the course of an action that traces American involvement in Vietnam, from induction into the army through unspeakable cruelties on both sides to the final circle of corpses, 'the reverse of the beautiful circle of the opening image'. Built on group improvisation, free in its transformations, the play does not accomplish Terry's stated objective of 'getting at the essence of violence', but it does present strong group images.

Even before the Open Theatre disbanded in 1973, Megan Terry brought their improvisation techniques to other theatres, professional and amateur. In co-operation with students at the innovative Immaculate Heart College of Los Angeles, she developed her *Tommy Allen Show*. *Approaching Simone* was written for the Boston University centennial in 1970, but it also marks a break with Terry's parodies of the 1960s, since Simone Weil is a wholly sympathetic protagonist. Terry's staging is quite elaborate as she traces Weil's life from childhood to willed martyrdom. As a child, Simone carries heavy burdens, spurns stockings because the poor lack them, and refuses sugar because soldiers are short of it. At fourteen she is tempted by suicide but rises above it: 'Focus on the dark inside your head.' As an adult she dances with a black American singer. She is twice discharged from teaching positions for dedication beyond the classroom, and she turns happily to factory work.

Act I might be called the Abjuration of Self, with Act II the Immersion in Community – a union activist in her factory, a volunteer in the Spanish Civil War, a Christian inspired by the poems of George Herbert, a Jewish refugee in Marseille, a participant in Harlem gospel services, and finally a London volunteer for the Free French during the Second World War. Assigned to clerical work rather than the dangerous mission she requests, Simone starves herself to death, refusing food as she once refused sugar unavailable to her compatriots.

Terry's modesty is evident in her title *Approaching Simone*, but her saint is less dramatic than Corneille's Polyeucte or Eliot's Thomas, for Simone faces small opposition to her dedication. Terry's scenic images are inventive: the elaborate planes against which the action unfolds; white poultices of increasing size, physicalising Simone's self-doubt; the activities of Simone's students, who recite and hike through the audience; human machines in the factory; revolving pyramids as Simone lectures; Chorus members donning Simone's garments as they fall; the increasingly tall and fat figures of the Free French in London; the transformation of the Chorus into a pile of war corpses; and, finally, Simone's ascent to sainthood.

Terry's next extended drama, *Hothouse* (1974), is

thought to show that 'strength is passed down from one woman to another', but the play actually rollicks through three generations of hard-drinking, hard-loving women joined in a thin plot and marred by what is unusual in Terry's full-length plays – obedience to old conventions of family realism. Back at her home base of Omaha Magic Theatre, Terry presented that theatre's most popular piece, *Babes in the Bighouse, a Documentary Musical Fantasy about Life in a Women's Prison* (1974). Blending documentary research, the cell effects of the Living Theatre *Frankenstein*, and Open Theatre transformations, Terry examines a special feminist area – prison. With neither the relentless brutality of *The Brig* nor the simulated torture of realistic stage jails, *Babes in the Bighouse* stages the abyss between behaviour and punishment, desire and fulfilment, loneliness and enforced company. Without linear plot, the three men and three women ('babes' are played by both sexes) transform in several roles based on improvisations, but they nevertheless trace continuous prison life.

Co-operating willingly with prisoners, students or feminists, Terry worked with the last group on dramatising the sexism of the English language. *American Kings English for Queens* (1978) is a witty but confusing title, since 'queens' in today's slang means male homosexuals and not women, much less feminists. Through scenes centred on the family, that bourgeois cell that was anathema in the 1960s, the masculinity of the English language is depicted. Adopting the feral child Morgan, the family's oldest daughter realises, 'We'll have to think of a way we can teach her to talk without making her feel that being a girl is not as good as being a boy.' With the help of music, a cranky, and stage animality, the family succeed theatrically, if not humanistically, since the play ends in song, 'When is a human being, Being a human being?'

Although *Attempted Rescue on Avenue B* (1979) is subtitled 'A Beat Fifties Comic Opera', it is actually a realistic play set in New York City's East Village between 1958 and 1960. Actress Mira Anderson moves into the small Avenue B apartment of painter Landy Taverniti. The play traces their craggy relationship, as well as the demands of their respective arts, as Terry evokes Bohemia in the 1950s, down to the Abstract Expressionist process of painting and the Method explorations of acting. In a larger context *Rescue* is Terry's attempt to rescue the avant-garde of the 1950s from contempt at the end of the 1970s.

More obstreperously feminist is *Mollie Bailey's Traveling Circus: Featuring Scenes from the Life of Mother Jones* (1983). Terry interweaves actual biographical details about the labour organiser Mother Jones with the story of a fictional Mollie Bailey, her imagined contemporary. Through her juxtaposition of Bailey's family 'circus' and Jones's public dedication, Terry points up the value of both and re-views history as her-story – in celebration.

Versatile, energetic, endlessly inventive, Megan Terry has created many many plays that have provided pleasure and/or instruction to different co-workers and many kinds of audiences. Often vividly immediate, her plays rarely attain the fusion of phrase to image which distinguishes durable drama.

Less prolific, Maria Irene Fornès has also enhanced the Off-Off-Broadway scene with several talents. Of Cuban birth (in 1930), she is doubly trilingual: she speaks Spanish, English and French, and her artistic languages are designing, directing and playwriting. Her two volumes of published plays (a selection culled from some two dozen) show meticulous attention to visual as well as verbal detail.

Never realistic, Fornès's plays offer an oblique critique of the reality of the emotions.

Her first play announces the light touch of her first volume. Although developed traditionally for the Actor's Workshop of San Francisco, *Tango Palace* (1961) displays her delight in acting, rather than plot or character development. The tango palace designates the habitat and shrine of Isidore, '*an androgynous clown*', who is accosted by an earnest youth, Leopold. Leopold is a rationalist, seeking logic and sequence, whereas the inventive Isidore moves through roles by caprice. The action of *Tango Palace* pivots on the duel of Isidore and Leopold. When Leopold refuses to continue their duel, he plunges a sword into Isidore, who promptly appears as an angel, still carrying aphorisms on cards. The play ends when '*Leopold walks through the door slowly, but with determination. He is ready for the next stage of their battle.*'

Fornès's *The Successful Life of 3* (1965) was created with the Open Theatre, thriving on humour and spurning psychology in an extended pun on an eternal triangle. He and She are a couple, and a rival, 3, vies for She's love. The play traces their intertwined lives from first meeting in a doctor's office, where She is a nurse, through the marriage of He and She, the desertion of He by She, She's return to a household of He and 3, the arrest of 3 (as thief) by He (as detective) and 3's adventures with police and bodyguards, to a final joyous reunion of the three.

Promenade was written soon after *The Successful Life of 3*, presenting the zany adventures of two triangles – the prisoners 105 and 106 and their mother, on the one hand, and the same men with a female companion, on the other. After digging their way out of prison, the two men attend a banquet, where they steal everything portable, including a woman whom they drape in their loot.

Suddenly, they are joined by their mother to comfort soldiers on a battlefield. Then they are imprisoned again, along with mother and woman. Finally alone in jail, they sing: 'All is well in the city ... And for those who have no cake, / There's plenty of bread.'

With *Dr Kheal* (1968) Fornès's satire becomes more overt. Like Dr Kheal's predecessors, Ionesco's teacher in *The Lesson* and Adamov's Professor Taranne, Fornès's professor takes a stance of omniscience, which is shaken in the play's action. Unlike his forerunners, however, Dr Kheal unbalances his *own* omniscience, with the self-contradiction implicit in his name (containing 'heal' and 'kill'): '[Reality] is opposites, contradictions compressed so that you don't know where one stops and the other begins.'

In *Molly's Dream* (1968) Fornès for the first time presents a rational structure for her surreal associations. The action is set in an old-fashioned saloon where waitress Molly looks at a young man. She leans her head on a table, falls asleep, and dreams most of the rest of the play, which gradually narrows down to herself and the young man as Jim. Although he leaves the saloon before she awakens, she gazes at the spot where he sat – now empty of the several whimsical characters of popular culture.

During the 1970s Fornès's administrative work for New York's Theatre Strategy reduced her time for playwriting. Of three plays of these years – *The Curse of the Langston House* (1972), *Aurora* (1973) and *Fefu and her Friends* (1977) – the last is widely viewed as a new direction for Fornès. The audience is divided into four groups, who move through the rooms of a New England country house: living-room to lawn to study to bedroom to kitchen and back to living-room, there to watch scenes between Fefu, nickname for Stephany Beckman, and her seven women friends, on a spring day in 1935.

Aside from hostess Fefu (married to Phillip, who never appears), there is Julia in her wheelchair, the pair Christina and Cindy, histrionic Emma, ex-lovers Paula and Cecilia, and helpful Sue. Fefu has been toying with a gun before her guests arrive. The purpose of the women's meeting is to raise funds for supporting art as a tool of learning, with actual quotations from 'The Science of Educational Dramatics' by Emma Sheridan Fry. As the offstage women laughingly engage in a water-fight, Fefu is quite suddenly brutal to Julia, insisting that she can walk, that she can combat the deadly forces that she hallucinates. Interrupted by Christina, Fefu takes her gun outside. A shot is soon heard, and Fefu re-enters with a dead rabbit, to utter the play's closing line: 'I killed it ... I just shot ... and killed it ... Julia.' The others surround the bleeding Julia as the light fades.

Wounded though she is, perhaps dead, Julia triumphs over Fefu, whose hesitancies cast doubt on her ability to kill 'it'. Although the innovative staging calls for the audience participation that was a tenet of the 1960s, the play is true to Fornès's own major theme – the triumph of the irrational. Through a darker environment, Fefu and Julia continue the duel of Leopold and Isidore of *Tango Palace* into '*the next stage of their battle*'.

Since *Molly's Dream* in 1968, Fornès has been directing the first productions of her plays, often beginning rehearsals with an incomplete script. Although the settings of her plays have become increasingly diverse, they resemble one another in steady focus on the inner life of her characters. In the first volume of her plays that life is rendered playfully, often with song and dance. The second volume is not only more painful, but more aware of a global context for private lives. *Fefu* is the transitional play, blending the playfulness of the lesser characters into the ultimately lethal game of Fefu, the ebullience of Emma's drama lesson into Julia's obsession with death. Eight women meet to rehearse a programme about the instructional power of art, and we are present at their meeting to be instructed by Fornès's art. In a typically brilliant sentence of Susan Sontag, 'Character is revealed through catechism' in Fornès's plays, but questions dominate answers in the more recent plays.

Sontag's introduction to Fornès's plays of the 1980s cogently asserts that they present 'both a theatre about utterance (i.e., a metatheatre) and a theatre about the disfavored'. And both theatres make their points theatrically, with considerable subtlety. Thus *Danube* (1982) moves inexorably from Ionesco-type phrases of language-learning to a nuclear winter, which is never designated but only suffered. *Mud* (1983), as Sontag points out, contrasts with an earlier Fornès play in that it dramatises the *un*successful life of three, since Mae, in contrast to both her lovers, strives to learn her way up out of the ubiquitous mud. Although she is shot to prevent her departure – 'Where I don't have my blood sucked' – she is aware of the meaning of her death. So, too, in *Sarita* (1984), the protagonist resembles the earlier Molly in her passionate subservience to a man. But Molly whiles her passion away on filmic dreams, whereas Sarita stabs her faithless lover – and thereby loses her own identity. Molly's old-fashioned timeless saloon fragments into a series of painful places for Sarita, who is so immersed in her own emotional fray that she is unaware of the Second World War raging around her.

Abingdon Square (1984) is Jamesian not only in title but in its quiet study of intimate relations in early-twentieth-century New York City. Fifteen-year-old Marion marries fifty-year-old Juster, whose son Michael is the same age as Marion. Eventually and inevitably, Marion takes a lover, and during the First World War Juster exiles her from their home and child. When Juster has a stroke, Marion returns to nurse him. Finally, all passions are spent – when Marion is twenty-four years old. Without the labyrinthine Jamesian syntax, Fornès confronts her characters with feelings that are known only when verbalised. Good people all, they wound one another tenderly.

Like many women playwrights, Maria Irene Fornès has been claimed by feminists, and she does reveal deep sympathy for old servant women, or women who seek wisdom, or passionate women who reject enslavement to sexuality – even through murder. But *Fefu* alone is wholly feminine in the drama of a playwright whose affection for her characters never dribbles into sentimentality.

This chapter has grouped a few playwrights who began Off-Off-Broadway, and who have worked closely with actors. Although Jack Gelber now reads like a traditionalist, he joined the Living Theatre when the Becks were formulating the radical aesthetic that influenced theatres around the world. (I shall glance in the next chapter at their collective plays.) The Living Theatre's most methodical non-Method actor, Joe Chaikin, founded the Open Theatre with the actor at its aesthetic centre, but the group welcomed the assistance of other theatre artists, including playwrights. Jean-Claude van Itallie, Megan Terry, Irene Fornès produced a body of plays seeded by actors' exercises, particularly transformation. At the same time, in neighbouring unconventional spaces, other actors deliberately cultivated a rough style or emotional crescendos, which are reflected in plays of Israel Horovitz. The Open Theatre was almost alone in *disciplining* the heterogeneous energies of Off-Off-Broadway in the 1960s, but the movement inevitably fell prey to attack by time. As young theatre amateurs grew older, they moved in the 1970s either toward professionalism or, more often, away from the theatre. A very small percentage persisted in their craft, which involved its own transformations in the 1980s.

6
Agit-Prop and Political Purpose: the Becks, Holden, Valdez, Nelson

In 1968, the Year of the Radical, a new KKK threatened the land in the Killing of King and Kennedy. One of the year's less violent events was the birth of the Radical Theatre Repertory, which proclaimed,

> The member groups, and dozens of others in this country and abroad, are in the vanguard of a new phenomenon in theatrical and social history – the spontaneous generation of communal playing troupes, sharing voluntary poverty, making experimental collective creations and exploring space, time, minds, and bodies in manifold new ways to meet the demands of our explosive period.

With the exception of the Firehouse Theatre in Minneapolis (but soon thereafter in San Francisco), the nineteen radical groups of the Repertory were located on the two coasts of the United States, thirteen in New York. Although the members agreed on opposition to the war in Vietnam, over half of them were not overtly political.

A decade afterwards, six of the nineteen groups were still playing, and only three were politically radical – the Living Theatre, the San Francisco Mime Troupe and El Teatro Campesino.

The 'new phenomenon' was not quite new, for 'communal playing troupes' date back to the Russian Revolution. The phrase 'agit-prop' comes from Russia: the *Oxford English Dictionary* records its earliest use in 1934, as a derivative of the Russian *agitatsiya-propaganda*: 'A department of the Central Committee of the Russian Communist Party responsible . . . for "agitation and propaganda" on behalf of Communism.' An easily naturalised phrase, agit-prop early sought theatre outlets. In the 1930s – the period that director Harold Clurman called 'the fervent years' – American agit-prop theatre sprang up in unions, neighbourhoods, and the federally financed Works Project Administration; sprang up and often collapsed with the moment's crisis. Nevertheless, such theatre led to the formation of the Actor's Studio and the Method-acting empire, which later penetrated all countries through Hollywood films. Few contemporary American actors are unmarked by acting styles of the fervent years. In that period drama also broadened its subject matter and occasionally its idiom. Playwrights Robert Ardrey, Paul Green, Lillian Hellman, Clifford Odets, Elmer Rice, William Saroyan and Irwin Shaw were nurtured by the radical theatre of the 1930s, though the production process was traditional enough: the playwright would deliver a script, which the director would cast not only with actors but also with designers and technicians.

The radicals of the 1960s often rejected specialisation, including that of the writer. The Radical Repertory credo of 1968 speaks of 'exploring space, time, minds, and bodies', but not language. And yet political radicals were less suspicious of words than performance radicals in the wake of Artaud. Politically radical theatres deploy words in two main ways – either as weapons hurled at the audience or as invitations to communal laughter at satirised villains.

The Living Theatre achieved international celebrity through its assault arsenal. Ardent pacifists, Julian Beck and Judith Malina shared an embattled life. Meeting in 1943 while still in their teens, founding a theatre in 1947, they staged non-commercial plays by W. H. Auden, Bertolt Brecht, Jean Cocteau, Paul Goodman, Federico García Lorca, Gertrude Stein and W. C. Williams. Their *succès de scandale*, as discussed in the last chapter, is associated with two playwrights whom they produced in the early 1960s – Jack Gelber's junkie *Connection* and Kenneth Brown's Marine *Brig*. Revolting against theatre conventions for these radical scripts, the Becks infused their Living Theatre with a new vision – living as theatre and theatre as living. Never was a theatre more presciently named. Until Beck's death in 1985 the couple were tireless leaders, speakers, performers. They were arrested, beaten, adored and sometimes subsidised. Judith Malina and Julian Beck became familiar names to people who had never seen them in the flesh. They were photographed dirty, naked, maniacal, and yet they retained their dignity. No one called them Judie and Julie.

Optimistically Beck hoped, 'The theater is the Wooden Horse by which we can take the town.' It is easy today to sneer that no town has been taken by these combative anarchists. But the Becks captured the imagination of a young generation in the 1960s; their Wooden Horse was personal example, including the example of public performance. Their martyrdom began in 1963, when their

1. Playwright Neil Simon

2. *Duck Variations* by David Mamet. Photo: Ron Blanchette

3. *Alfred Dies* by Israel Horovitz. Photo: Ron Blanchette

4. *The Connection* by Jack Gelber. Photo: © Alix Jeffry 1981/Harvard Theatre Collection

5. *Motel* by Jean-Claude van Itallie. Photo: Niblock/Bough

6. *Bag Lady* by Jean-Claude van Itallie. Photo: Nathaniel Tileston

7. Playwright Amiri Baraka (LeRoi Jones)

8. *Dutchman* by LeRoi Jones. Photo: © Alix Jeffry 1981/Harvard Theatre Collection

9. *The Corner* by Ed Bullins. Photo: Friedman-Abeles

10. *Funnyhouse of a Negro* by Adrienne Kennedy. Photo: © Alix Jeffry 1981/Harvard Theatre Collection

11. *Bluebeard* by Charles Ludlam. Photo: Thomas Harding

12. *The Moke-Eater* by Kenneth Bernard. Photo: Robert A. Propper

13. *Night Club* by Kenneth Bernard. Photo: Allan Tepper

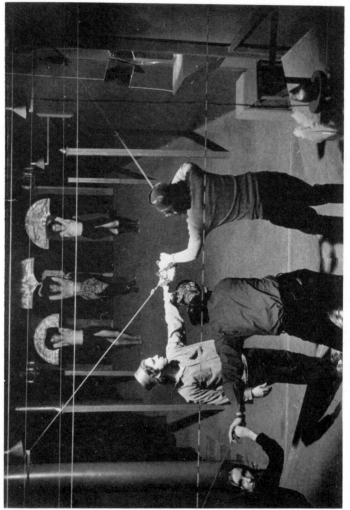

14. *Pandering to the Masses: A Misrepresentation* by Richard Foreman. Photo: Theodore Shank

15. *The Red Horse Animation* by Lee Breuer. Photo: Theodore Shank

16. Playwright Sam Shepard. Photo: Ron Blanchette

17. *The Tooth of Crime* by Sam Shepard. Photo: Ron Blanchette

18. *Angel City* by Sam Shepard. Photo: Ron Blanchette

New York City theatre was padlocked for non-payment of taxes, although they charged that the true cause was performance of the anti-militarist *Brig*. For five years after that, they and their company wandered around Europe, collaborating on creations in thirteen different countries. Although few of these creations originated in words, the scripts were later published, and it is by virtue of such publication that the theatrical Becks may be classified as dramatists.

Mysteries and Smaller Pieces (1964) consists of a dozen scenes, and words are uttered – sparingly – in only three; they figure importantly in only one – 'Street Songs'. The scenic directions indicate the new performance strategy of the Living Theatre:

> No curtain.
> Performers circulate among audience. Everyday clothes.
> Performers become part of audience.
> Contacts.

'Contacts' rarely meant words. The first silent scene recapitulates *The Brig*, with its inhuman imposition of mechanical motions. In the second scene, 'The Dollar Poem', the words on a dollar are recited chorally to strict choreography. An Indian *raga* is followed by wordless processions of performers among spectators. In 'Street Songs' two-beat agitational slogans are chanted in random order by a single actor, and these words are echoed by performers seated among the spectators. When these actors move to the stage, still chanting, they invite the audience to join them in a large circle. Everyone hums, breathes, exercises rhythmically.

After an intermission, the actors perform intricate *tab-*

leaux vivants with rectangular white boxes. They then pass sound and gesture from individual to individual. These 'smaller pieces' prepare the final scene of an Artaudian plague, a mystery. Each performer enacts a death by plague. In Leslie Epstein's description, 'A body shudders, a mouth opens, closes, a rattle, a sigh, silence around me now, people fall from their seats, kneel by the dying, embrace them.' When the company lies rigid and scattered, 'survivors' carry the 'corpses' centre stage, remove their shoes, stroke contorted limbs, and pile them neatly one on top of another, five on the bottom layer, then four, three, two and one. At the last we behold a harmonious pyramid.

The next two productions of the Living Theatre retreated to fiction – *Frankenstein* (1965) and *Antigone* (1966), adapted to emphasise the repressive evil of a dominant class. After these performances, the company felt imprisoned by scripts. *Paradise Now* (1968) was therefore a deliberate return to the verbal paucity and ritual gestures of *Mysteries*. Unlike the fairly discrete scenes of *Mysteries*, however, *Paradise Now* is meant to be a continuous journey, which is also a 'trip'. There are eight stages or processes to the journey, each with its own Rite, Vision, and Action. (These are the published titles, but it was hard in performance to differentiate Rite from Vision or mere image.) A blend of dark night of the soul, Kabbala, *I Ching* and Tantric Buddhism, the performance lasted four to five hours, and always lost spectators before the end. Rites and Visions were performed for spectators, but Actions were an open invitation for audience participation. Rung IV, entitled 'Universal Intercourse', was sensational in 1968; certain spectators enthusiastically entered an orgy while others departed in disgust. By Rung VIII the participants of the new Paradise moved out into the open air.

In spite of the title – *Paradise Now* – the performance was most forceful in infernos, when the theatre crowd was harassed by repressive agents but shouted defiantly, 'Free theatre. The theatre is yours. Act. Speak. Do whatever you want.'

Having asserted freedom in *Paradise Now*, the Living Theatre turned its collective back on formal theatres. In 1970 the collective divided into four groups in four countries. The Beck portion went to São Paulo, Brazil, where it conceived an ambitious project, *The Legacy of Cain*, a performance cycle that was envisioned as growing to 150 pieces. Deported from Brazil to the United States, the Beck Living Theatre at first engaged in agit-prop on current issues, especially the Vietnam War, but by 1973 it developed the first extended spectacle of the *Cain* cycle, *Seven Meditations on Political SadoMasochism*. Malina wrote the first meditation, and the group chose other texts to form the basis of the remaining six. In contrast to the confrontation tactics of the 1960s, the actors encircled the audience in a collective embrace.

At the company headquarters in Brooklyn toward the end of 1973, the group began work on another *Cain* piece, *The Money Tower*, which, ironically, was funded by the Mellon Foundation. Physical structure and scenario displayed the hierarchy of the *Cain* society – the audience's own. As in 'Street Songs' from *Mysteries*, the words are changed: 'This is the House that money built.' Occasionally, sentences recall the hopeful 1930s: 'The workers will organise the work and there will be no more money and no more money system and we will all be free.' Moving to Pittsburgh in 1974, the Living Theatre performed another piece of the *Cain* cycle, *Six Public Acts to Transmute Violence into Concord*. The title indicates how far the Becks had travelled from the furious 1960s, but they were nevertheless faithful to their creed of political anarchy and biomechanical aesthetics.

In 1975 the Becks started on what they anticipated as a European tour, but it turned out to be extended exile, with occasional subsidy in Rome and Paris. They sporadically added pieces to the *Cain* cycle, as well as reworking *Prometheus* (1979). The rebel god becomes the American anarchist Alexander Berkman, and Io becomes Emma Goldman, very different from that of Rochelle Owens. The whole looks back on the Becks' 1950s taste for plays within plays, since the director of this *Prometheus* is Lenin, played by Beck. Faithful to the participatory aesthetics of the 1960s, the performance forces an audience to choose sides in the storming of the Russian Winter Palace.

After a decade the Becks brought the Living Theatre (with a new generation of actors) back to New York City. Beck appeared in several film roles and wrote the script *The Archaeology of Sleep;* he seemed at the height of his considerable creative powers when he died of cancer in 1985. Judith Malina announced that the Living Theatre would continue, under her direction and that of long-time member Hanon Reznikov.

In its unique history, the Living Theatre has encouraged few living playwrights. After *Paradise Now*, however, the Becks freely offered their nominally collective scripts to anyone who wished to perform them: 'The play "Paradise Now" is not private property: / there are no performance royalties to pay: / it is free: / for any community that wants to play it.' Other communities have occasionally performed Living Theatre scripts, but without the same impact.

Two other long-term radical theatres offer scripts that have been performed widely. In 1968 a radical theatre festival was held at San Francisco State University, involving three groups – Peter Schuman's Bread and Puppet Theatre, Ronnie Davis's San Francisco Mime Troupe, and Luis Valdez's Teatro Campesino, each dominated by the strong personality of its founding father. Unlike New York's Living Theatre, the San Francisco Mime Troupe and El Teatro Campesino perform in California's mild climate. Moreover, their propaganda beguiles audiences with no experience of theatre, since their main genre is broad comedy.

The San Francisco Mime Troupe was founded in 1959 by Ronnie Davis, who had trained as a mime artist. During the 1960s the loosely organised but very vocal troupe hesitated between enacting political sketches and staging aesthetic events. By 1967 the group had evolved a modified *commedia* style for park performance, and radical politics triumphed over radical aesthetics. Performances were short, pungent, and penned by any writer corralled by Davis. In 1970 a cohesive theatre group declared itself a collective whose main purpose was to perform political plays in Bay Area parks. Davis resigned.

This collective was in no sense an imitation of the Living Theatre. The members did not live communally, and they did not claim universal theatre skills. Rather, they were a political and economic collective, each member drawing the same salary but exercising his or her main skill. Most of the members were performers, but a non-performer, Joan Holden, gradually evolved as the company's main dramatist; she is given at least partial credit for six of the eight plays published in the troupe anthology *By Popular Demand*.

Unlike Holden's adaptations under the aegis of Ronnie Davis, *The Independent Female* (1970) was patterned on melodrama rather than *commedia*. Both forms manipulate the old formula of Greek New Comedy – a pair of lovers overcoming an obstacle to their union. In *commedia* the obstacle is a stock comic – Pantalone, Il Dottore, Il Capitano. In the Mime Troupe's modified *commedia* these masked acrobatic figures are satirised representatives of capitalism, but in Holden's modified melodrama the obstacle is a young woman's nascent independence. When the heroine's friend, a veteran feminist, is killed – 'My epitaph: "Shot in her back for refusing to live on it"' – the *ingénue* resolutely rejects her sexist lover. Holden's happy ending is not the traditional coupling, but a determined sisterhood of independent females.

As Holden's *Independent Female* (1970) subverts soap opera, her *Dragon Lady's Revenge* (1971) subverts the comic strip (*Terry and the Pirates*) to condemn US intervention in the 'fictional' land of Long Penh, a punning reference to Vietnam: 'Basically, we are here because we desperately want to get out!' Similarly, *San Fran Scandals* (1973, composed with fellow Trouper Steve Friedman) subverts musical comedy to expose the scandalous greed of real-estate operators at the expense of the aged and indigent; *Frijoles* (1975) subverts farce in revealing how multinational trusts exploit workers in both the United States and the Third World, even to robbing them of *frijoles* or the dietary staple of beans; and *Mozamgola Caper*, (1987) subverts the spy thriller in order to expose US involvement in South African apartheid.

In the 1980s Holden wrote a trilogy of plays with the same central protagonist. In *Factperson* (1980) the person of the title is an old baglady with the power to cite facts that contradict the lies of the media. Since such lies were and are ubiquitous, the resulting play was confusing, and Holden soon focused her satire on the fundamentalist Moral Majority. The old baglady became a Spirit of Information, who endows an old wino with her telling facts.

This gives Factwino the power to make people *think* – a power that he retains only when sober: 'If you booze it, you lose it'. Though temporarily triumphant, Factwino is captured by a fearful two-headed monster, Armageddonman. Like a Superman comic strip, this play ends in suspense, with Factwino's fate in doubt.

In *Factwino vs. Armageddonman* (1982) 'the double-headed dealer of doom' or the military–industrial powers keep Factwino submissive with drink. However, another wino tracks down his buddy and heroically liberates him. Although these two popular plays (with musical accompaniment and clever songs) revert to comic-strip technique, the third play in the sequence, *Factwino: the Opera* (1985), reflects a shift in Holden's dramaturgy which she dates from *False Promises* (1976).

For that play Holden did research into American underground history – the contributions of labour, women, minorities, rather than big names – to achieve heightened realism in characters who fought their way up from under. Similarly, the final view of Factwino humanises him. No longer a Superman clone, Factwino is revealed as Sedro F. Wooley, a radical newscaster who became a wino when he was fired. Since the Spirit of Information spurns miracles, Wooley develops his own strength and serves as an example to others: 'Everybody has to find their own power.'

Less agit-prop than these summaries may sound, Holden's scripts are invincibly funny and celebratory, with audiences hissing the villains but sharing the confusions of the increasingly realistic working-class characters. In this vein her deepest play to date is *Steeltown* (1984), which moves from a disillusioned present to a hopeful past. Thus the first act is farce, and the second a romantic musical. Act I recalls the frenzy of factory work in Chaplin's *Modern*

Times. Steelworkers, smitten with contemporary consumerism, betray their union to overwork for overtime pay. Aware of this dehumanisation, a Steeltown wife leaves her husband. Act II moves us back to 1945, full of hope after the Second World War. That act (and the play) ends on a strong union and the marriage of the couple who separate in Act I. Not only do all have to find their own power, but in this consumer society they can lose it even without booze.

Like Brecht, Holden views her plays as *Versuche*, experiments subject to change in performance – not only in rehearsal but also in actual performance, which she attends assiduously. The antithesis of a lonely writer dependent on inspiration, she visualises particular Mime Troupe actors speaking her lines, even though the lines may actually fall to others. When Holden talks about her plays, she speaks of *scripting* rather than writing; plays may form in several heads, but her own two hands pound out the words of a playable draft – playable by other troupes as well as the Mime Troupe.

Luis Valdez, founder of El Teatro Campesino, worked earlier with the Mime Troupe. Born into a large family of migrant farmworkers in 1940, Valdez did not learn English until he attended school in California. As a child, he was fascinated by puppets and school plays. On scholarship at San Jose State University, he read plays omnivorously and worked at the first of several versions of his *Shrunken Head of Pancho Villa*. While many of his family were active in the California grape strike, he continued to play at his plays – until Davis's Mime Troupe performed on the San Jose campus. Magnetised by their lively style, he joined the Troupe. When he marched with the strikers he was encouraged by President Chavez of the United Farmworkers to found a farmworkers' theatre.

Armed with signs reading *Huelgista* (striker), *Esquirol* (strike-breaker), *Patroncito* (grower), and *Contractista* (contractor), Valdez asked workers to enact these roles of their daily experience; their colleagues became audience and critics. Picketing all day, the farmworker–actors rehearsed at night and performed weekly in *actos* which Valdez wrote not merely about but for the workers. Enacting daily union events, the skits could be in Spanish, English, or the mixture called Spanglish. Sometimes actors played at union headquarters in Delano, California, but more often on the flatbed of a truck driven right up to the picket line.

The union won its strike, and in 1976 El Teatro Campesino travelled across the country, playing union halls and more commercial venues. Back in California, Valdez moved his company away from union headquarters to establish El Centro Campesino Culturál, an organisation to encourage Chicanos to take a pride in their cultural heritage. By 1968 other Chicano theatre groups had sprung up in the south-western United States and Latin America, forming TENAZ, Teatro Nacionál de Aztlan. In 1970 the Centro bought 40 acres in the California mission town of San Juan Bautista and established a cultural and agricultural collective. A packing warehouse was converted into a theatre.

Like the Living Theatre and the San Francisco Mime Troupe, El Teatro Campesino starts a new work with group discussion, but *actos* started with discussions based on the day's picketing. Gradually, the *actos* became more sophisticated; signs were replaced by masks and skilled physicality; solutions were not always evident.

In 1971 El Teatro Campesino published a volume of nine *actos* written between 1965 and 1971 by 'Luis Valdez y el Teatro Campesino', Valdez relinquishing his anonymity. Of the nine, only three deal with farm labour problems. Two examine the problematic role of Chicanos in the Vietnam War. A puppet play portrays the Aztec history of Mexico, and three plays deal with *La Raza* in a way that predicts the new form of *mito* (myth) developed by Valdez, dramatising Aztec and Mayan myths.

The only transplant from the 1965 picket line is *Las dos caras del patroncito* ('The Two Faces of the Boss'). Basically a vaudeville skit in which the Boss and the farmworker exchange clothes and attitudes, it points out that attitude is locked into social class.

La quinta temporada ('The Fifth Season', 1966) is more sustained. A farmworker, exploited both by Boss and Contractor, lives precariously through the four seasons, which are personified by actors. Summer is dressed like an ordinary farmworker, but his clothes are covered with paper money. Fall is also covered with money, but more sparsely. Winter is a monster who seizes money from everyone in sight. Spring rescues the mistreated farmworker, indoctrinates him with union slogans, but disappears all too soon. By the time Summer and Fall reappear with their temptations, the farmworker has gone on strike. Winter then attacks the Grower, who is rescued only when he consents to a union contract. Winter's sign gives way to that of the fifth season – social justice.

One of the most popular *actos* on university campuses is *Los vendidos* ('The Sell-outs', 1967). Miss Jimenez of the State Government shops in Honest Sancho's Used Mexican Lot for a token brown face to display in government offices. She rejects made-in-Mexico candidates in favour of a Mexican-American who snaps to her commands. But then he unexpectedly incites his fellow Mexicans to revolution: '*The three models join together and advance toward the secretary who backs up and runs out of the shop screaming.'* Relieving 'Honest' Sancho of his profit, the three are not sell-outs, and they go to a party. (This *acto* was televised nationally.)

The longest *acto* in the collection, *No saco nada de la escuela* ('I Don't Get anything Out of School', 1969) traces black, white, and Chicano students through three stages of school – elementary, high and university – to show that Anglo education educates for an Anglo world. Similarly, the Vietnam *actos* show the folly of Chicano soldiers fighting for Anglo superiority in the United States.

Soldado Razo ('Chicano Soldier', 1971) opens with Chicano Johnny's death in Vietnam, and moves through flashback scenes linked by the visible presence of Death as a character. That figure darkens Johnny's pre-war exchanges with family and fiancée. Johnny is killed before he can reveal the full horror of the Vietnam War; his body is shipped home, and a pensive family in mourning files past his bier, questioning the need for such death. Although grouped with the *actos*, *Soldado Razo* indicates the path of Valdez's *mitos*, no longer agit-prop.

Few of the *mitos* have as yet been published, but *The Dark Root of a Scream* illustrates the form and, following *Soldado Razo*, shows the continuity of Valdez's evolution. The *acto* is a flashback series from a death in Vietnam; the *mito* is an emblematic spectrum of reactions to a death in Vietnam. Both plays implicitly decry Chicano acceptance of a sacrificial role. Death is the only non-realistic character of the *acto*, whereas the *mito* is rooted in its hero's transcendence. His name, Quetzalcoatl Gonzales, significantly combines the Aztec and Spanish elements of the Chicano's heritage.

What *acto* and *mito* both reject is European proscenium theatre. In Valdez's words, 'Our rejection of white western European (*gavacho*) proscenium theatre makes the birth of new Chicano forms necessary – thus, *los actos y los mitos*; one through the eyes of man; the other, through the eyes of God.' Since it is the specific man Valdez who pens the *mitos* ostensibly 'through the eyes of God', he has been criticised both within and outside the Chicano community for betraying his initial radicalism. This charge has been levelled, too, against his *corrido* or musical epic of sixteenth-century Spain, containing many modern musical forms.

Mundo is described by Valdez as a Chicano mystery/ miracle play. It was conceived in 1972 and went through six main revisions by 1980. The story concerns Mundo Mata, a *barrio* (slum-district) Chicano, who dies of a drug overdose and sets out through the underworld in search of his pregnant wife, his grandparents and his friends. He relives incidents in the life of a *barrio* Chicano – dances, cruising, knife fights, hold-ups, receipt of welfare, freeway accident. He pleads with powerful men in the United States and Soviet Union, who are indifferent to his plight. Through music, dance and ritual, the dead Mundo is resurrected, as in the culture of pre-Columbian Indians to whom the Chicanos trace their heritage.

Zoot Suit (1978), commissioned by the director Gordon Davidson for the Los Angeles Mark Taper Forum, is based on the events in 1943 when American soldiers brutally quelled 'zoot-suit' riots in the Los Angeles *barrio*. A white court condemned seventeen Mexican-Americans to life imprisonment on a trumped-up murder charge. The case was appealed and won on the basis of evidence gathered by the Communist reporter Alice Bloomfield. In Valdez's play the defendant Henry Reyna, like his predecessor Mundo, undertakes a musical odyssey through the *barrio*. Alternately tempted and assailed, he ends in a triumph that has attracted both white and Chicano audiences in

Los Angeles, but not on Broadway. Valdez also directed the film *Zoot Suit*, which has not been widely distributed.

In the 1980s Valdez's prime interest was film rather than theatre, but he did write one play for the Los Angeles Theater Center – *I Don't Have to Show You No Stinkin' Badges* (1986). The line is addressed to Humphrey Bogart by a Mexican-American actor in *The Treasure of the Sierra Madre*, and it announces Valdez's theme, that Chicanos need no longer play bit parts in white culture. No one has contributed more than Valdez to pride in Chicano theatre, but his recent work seeks political power through the mass media.

Everyone will disapprove of closing this chapter on Richard Nelson (b. 1950), who is affiliated with no under-privileged group, who urges no social cause, and whose plays have been performed in regional and subsidised theatres. Nelson is that rare American playwright – one with a global perspective – and with each play he has probed more deeply into the questionable stance of the United States in world politics. A college graduate who has worked as literary adviser in several theatres, Nelson is an intellectual whose work confers humane status on that maligned class.

Nelson divides his plays into three groups: (1) plays for which he gathered material while a newspaper reporter; (2) plays revolving around mythic figures within an Ameri-can context; (3) plays dramatising the inextricability of pri-vate tension from public context. Through most of these plays runs a metaliterary thread knotted with concern for the power and weakness of words. Nelson's first volume of plays straddles the first and second groups. *Conjuring an Event* (1978) is a rather long-winded satire on how a 'factual' reporter learns to create news. *Bal* (1980) adapts Brecht's *Baal* to a contemporary context, and *The Return of Pinocchio* (1983) converts the puppet into a naïve but insensitive Italian-American, oblivious of the suffering in his native Italy.

In Nelson's third group of plays the characters are more incisively drawn, and the non-naturalistic techniques are less blatantly manipulated. *Vienna Notes* (1978) resembles *Conjuring an Event* in its manipulation of 'facts'. The reporter Charlie is, however, replaced by Senator Stubbs, who dictates the notes while he and his entourage are ambushed by terrorists in Vienna. Not only do his notes contradict the events we witness, but the Senator's pre-occupation with the durable record renders him insensitive to the human toll exacted.

With his plays of the 1980s Nelson abandons satire for more sympathetic characters, torn as they are between yearning and circumstance. In *Between East and West* (1984) a Czech director and his actress wife seek refuge in New York City. The husband embraces American vulgarity with its freedom, but the wife cannot adapt and returns to Prague. Zigzagging in time, the play also borrows Brecht-style projected scene-titles, which waver, however, between information and ironic commentary.

Principia Scriptoriae (1986) shifts the political background from Eastern Europe to an unnamed Latin American country. Under a fascist regime in 1970 two young writers are jailed and tortured for distributing left-wing leaflets. One of them is native to the country, but a graduate of Cambridge University; the other is an American from the Mid-West. Fifteen years later the country is ruled by a left-wing dictator, and an international writers' committee comes to protest against the imprisonment of a right-wing poet. Grown older if not wiser, the two former prisoners meet again: Ernesto is secretary to the Minister of Culture, and Bill is a journalist accompanying the delegation. Living in different countries, they have travelled different paths from their naïve youth, so that the principles of writing referred to in the title, and again projected à la Brecht, are wholly ironic.

In *Sensibility and Sense* (1988) only the time of day and the year are projected since the action zigzags between 1985 and 1937. Unlike the decorous behaviour of Jane Austen's characters in *Sense and Sensibility*, that of Nelson's triangle is riddled with barbs, envy, affection and ambiguity. In a plot probably sparked by the feud between Lillian Hellman and Mary McCarthy, two left-wing ladies each in turn married to the same left-wing writer war to the death. One has written a book condemning her whole generation of armchair liberals, and the other is prepared to sue. The play is critical of all three major characters for action limited to words, and yet there is a certain admiration for those very words.

Some Americans Abroad (1989) takes American academics with their students on a theatre trip to London and Stratford. Incisively, it juxtaposes high art and low principles as the group reels from theatre to theatre, and from human predicament to provisional resolution. This time the projections designate well-worn places on the tourist trek in England, but Nelson's dialogue has been honed to surgical precision in its exposure of the anatomy of miseducation.

In contrast to Britain, where politics dominate recent serious dramaturgy, such playwrights receive small welcome in the United States. The Becks have written phrases to speak, rather than dramas. Joan Holden continues to adapt popular genres for radical causes espoused by the San Francisco Mime Troupe. Luis Valdez has contrasted the explosive 1960s to the implosive 1970s, but has not commented on the 1980s as a time for the mass media, the new genre for which he now writes. In that decade, however, Richard Nelson staged the plight of those committed to liberalism and culture – particularly verbal culture.

7
Black on Black: Childress, Baraka, Bullins, Kennedy

When the word 'black' dislodged 'negro', a radical self-examination was forced upon the United States, and this was reflected in theatre. Loraine Hansberry's *Raisin in the Sun* (1959) seemed to hold promise for negro playwrights as well as actors: her cast included actor–playwrights Ossie Davis, Lonne Elder, Douglas Turner Ward. Only two years later Jean Genet's *The Blacks* exploded Off-Broadway, with then-unknown performers who have since attained celebrity – Roscoe Lee Browne, Godfrey Cambridge, Charles Gordone, James Earl Jones, Cicely Tyson. By the end of the three-year run of *The Blacks* (with cast replacements), the Negro Ensemble Company had been founded and funded in New York City.

At the end of the 1960s Doris Abramson nevertheless concluded her study of negro drama, 'Negro playwrights are in the same position today that they were in yesterday. They must find patronage where they can and, having found it, present plays about Negroes to a predominantly white audience whose values their plays frequently attack.'

103

Substitute the word 'black' for 'negro', and the statement still holds true. With the exception of brave, short-lived theatres in the black ghetto, most black dramatists have continued to entertain predominantly white audiences whose values engulf them. Black playwrights find it harder than whites to survive in unsubsidised theatres; there is small middle-class support, and theatre is scarcely a necessity among those living marginally. And yet a generation of elder black playwrights – James Baldwin, Alice Childress, Langston Hughes, Loften Mitchell, Ted Shine – stubbornly wrote for the stage.

Alice Childress is only now being acclaimed for a lifetime of dedication to the theatre. Born in Charleston, South Carolina, in 1920, she was brought up in Harlem, where a story-telling grandmother nurtured her love of fiction. During the 1940s she acted in productions of the American Negro Theatre, and she wrote her first play, *Florence*, in 1949. The name character, a black actress struggling in New York, never appears, but her mother waits in a Jim Crow Southern station for the train that will carry her to Florence, with the intention of bringing her home to a more realistic calling. After a conversation with a 'liberal' white woman who is willing to recommend Florence as a maid, however, Mama changes her mind. 'Keep trying', she writes to Florence, her actress daughter.

Trouble in Mind (1955) again draws upon Childress's experience as an actress, since the play concerns a white director and a largely black cast in a melodrama about lynching. During the course of rehearsals friction increases between the white director and the middle-aged black actress who plays the mother of a young man threatened by a mob because he had the temerity to vote. The black actress questions both the motives of the director and the authenticity of the script. When she refuses to continue without crucial changes, the director fires her. The rest of the cast support her stand, and she carries the day. The show goes on in amity – at least temporarily.

Leaving theatre blacks for more deeply rooted scenes of black life, Childress wrote more moving plays. *Wedding Band* (1966) is the drama of a black–white couple in the South of 1918. A white baker, Herman, has been living for ten years with a black seamstress, Julia, and he gives her a gold wedding-band although in South Carolina they cannot be legally married. After a vituperative meeting between his mother and Julia, Herman buys two boat tickets to the North. But it is too late. Mortally ill, he expires in the arms of Julia, who refuses his mother's plea to have him carried 'home' to die. Giving the tickets and wedding-band to her neighbour, Julia feeds Herman's dying fantasy that they are on their way north. Although Childress is overexplicit about the racial antagonism in this small South Carolina town, she creates a vivid sense both of the black community and of white prejudices during the war to end wars.

Wine in the Wilderness (1969) conveys a different community – contemporary Harlem during a race riot. A black artist, Bill, is painting a triptych on African women entitled 'Wine in the Wilderness', a quotation from *Omar Khayyám*. Two of the three canvases are complete, but he needs a model for the third – 'as close to the bottom as you can get without crackin' up'. Friends bring Tommy, a woman factory worker who has been burned out of her home during the riot. Uneducated but shrewd, she at first has romantic designs on Bill, but when she learns her role in the triptych she asserts her independence. To Bill's credit, he recognises her grass-roots grit, and the play closes as he paints her as the centrepiece of the triptych.

Criticised by blacks for her sympathetic white char-

acters, criticised by feminists for her man-needing women,
Alice Childress has been impervious to fashion in her creation of characters – black and white, male and female –
who try to salvage dignity from a discouraging milieu: 'I
was lost but now I'm found.' Two black male playwrights
in the next generation are far more assertive of black independence and even aggression.

Amiri Baraka has been a beacon to his people. Born
Everett Leroi Jones in 1934, he early rebelled against his
middle-class Newark (New Jersey) environment. At How-
ard University he valued only the teaching of poet Sterling
Brown and sociologist E. Franklin Frazier. He dropped
out of the university to enlist in the Air Force, where he
read voraciously. At the end of his two-year tour of duty,
he reacted against order by plunging into the Bohemianism
of Greenwich Village, where he began to write in different
genres. Since then, he has undergone several changes of
belief and expression. Werner Sollors' study provides a
helpful chronology:

	Commitment	Aesthetic
1958–61	Aesthetic protest Beat Bohemianism	Expressive
1960–5	Political/ethnic protest New Left	Mimetic
1964–75	Black cultural nationalism Kawaida	Pragmatic
1974–	Marxism–Leninism–Maoism	Pragmatic

In each of these periods Baraka wrote plays, but his earliest
attempts are lost.

The Eighth Ditch (Is Drama) (1960) was later incorpor-
ated into Baraka's novel *The System of Dante's Inferno*.

106

The Florentine poet consigned false counsellors to the eighth ditch of his eighth infernal circle, and Baraka's false counsellor has a number instead of a name – 64 or 8 × 8. A seduction/rape of 46 by 64, *Eighth Ditch* seeks to shock by subject and language. Baraka has dismissed the play as 'foetus drama', and Sollors interprets it as two aspects of Baraka himself – the adolescent bourgeois 46 raped by the ghetto black 64. Published in a literary quarterly before it was produced by the Off-Off-Broadway Poets' Theatre, *Eighth Ditch* brought Baraka into conflict with the law. The periodical was confiscated, the Poets' Theatre was fined, and Baraka was taken to court, where he defended himself successfully. The experience spurred him to new shock tactics. Blasphemy, obscenity, iconoclasm are omnipresent in Baraka's four plays which gained him notoriety when they were performed in New York in 1964 – *The Baptism*, *The Toilet*, *Dutchman* and *The Slave*.

Set in a black Baptist church, *The Baptism* is sacrilegious. A Minister and a Bohemian Homosexual vie for the favours of an adolescent Boy seeking baptism. An Old Woman accuses the Boy of the sin of masturbation, but six girls worship him as the 'beautiful screw of the universe', then turn against him, lusting for a second crucifixion. Only the Homosexual objects to their attack, but he is easily conquered. The Boy slays his enemies with a silver sword, but a motorcycle Messenger summons him to his father, who is about to destroy the world 'as soon as the bars let out'. Refusing to forsake erring humanity, the Boy is knocked unconscious, to be carried off by the Messenger. The Homosexual wonders, 'What happened to that cute little religious fanatic?' When the play ends, the audience wonders too.

Continuing his infernal travels, Baraka set his next play,

The Toilet, in a stinking high-school latrine, where the characters excrete literally and symbolically. A duel takes place there between white James Karolis and black Ray Foots. When Karolis gains a choke hold on Foots, blacks enter the fray, punch Karolis unconscious and leave him inert. But Ray returns and cradles in his arms the head of his beloved enemy. The hero's name hints at Baraka's own ambivalence – the light Ray of love and the grounded Foots of macho pressure.

In the original production of *The Toilet* young actors orchestrated the ghetto obscenities. In Larry Rivers' sculpted latrine the adolescents jabbed, swore, pivoted, taunted, and collectively rose to an orgiastic riot. With an educational institution reduced to excrement, with sporting spirit crumbled to cruelty, with colour reversal for a lynch mob, *The Toilet* does not fit the love story to the race story.

Tenderness is mortally wounded in *Dutchman*, a hate drama that made Baraka famous when he was still Leroi Jones. The subway in summer – what Baraka describes as 'the flying underbelly of the city' – is his most telling dramatic inferno. A sober passenger, Clay, is seated in the speeding train. When it stops, he exchanges glances with a woman outside. When it starts up again, the woman, Lula, enters the car – a beautiful, scantily dressed white woman, eating an apple. She chooses a seat beside the well-dressed young black, accuses him of staring at her, and admits seeking him out. Lula banters with Clay before an abrupt racial taunt: 'I bet you never once thought you were a black nigger.' By the next act, the rest of the subway car is visible, the two are physically touching, and the flirtation takes the form of Lula's 'chronicle' of the evening ahead of them. As more passengers enter the car, Lula's actions grow manic, embarrassing Clay. She sings, twists, dances, and tries to make him dance with her. When he attempts to restrain her, she insults him: 'Screw yourself, Uncle Tom. Thomas Woolly-head.' While passengers laugh, Clay clubs a drunk, forces Lula to her seat and slaps her twice. He has shed his respectable carapace, and he launches into a monologue of rage. Eventually Lula says she has 'heard enough', and, when Clay bends over her to claim his belongings, she stabs him twice. Following her orders, the other passengers drag Clay's body out. Another young black enters, books under his arm, and sits a few seats behind Lula. They exchange looks.

The brilliance of *Dutchman* lies in a fusion of symbolism and realism. Act I catches the inter-racial banter of Bohemians. The setting, however, suggests the mythic, which is confirmed by the characters' names; the young black is *clay* in the hands of the Lulu–Lilith white woman, *la belle dame sans merci*. Thus prepared, Act II bursts out of psychological probability into myth – black against white, man against woman, private emotions against public spectacle. As Sherley Anne Williams showed, Baraka anchors his play in three myths: (1) 'the *Flying Dutchman* . . . roamed the seas and added unwary ships to its phantom entourage'; (2) 'a Dutch man-of-war . . . brought the first black slaves to North America'; and (3) 'the apples . . . seem to bear some resemblance to the biblical fruit of the tree of knowledge'. The white seductress tempts the slave's scion to self-knowledge, but with that knowledge comes death, and the ritual temptation–murder will be repeated eternally.

Of Baraka's four infernos of 1964, *The Slave* alone dramatises an inferno of the black protagonist's own making. Walker Vessels, a black leader in a race war, returns to the home of his white ex-wife and her liberal husband, formerly his literature professor. As the outside war draws

109

closer, the three insult one another, Walker drinking heavily. When the professor attempts to overpower Walker, the latter shoots him. Walker's wife Grace is fatally injured in an explosion, and he lets her die in the belief that their children are dead, but a child's screams are the last sounds before a final explosion.

In 1967 Leroi Jones became Imamu Amiri Baraka, a minister of the Kawaida faith. He then founded Spirit House, but his agit-prop plays predate the conversion. As mentioned in chapter 6, agit-prop tends to employ either shock techniques or broad satire. Baraka's plays shock. His anti-white rage flails out for a dramatic style. *Experimental Death Unit #1* (1965) begins as an absurdist dialogue between two white drug addicts vying for a black whore, but the black execution squad of the title slays all three, mounting the white heads on pikes. *A Black Mass* (1966) is science fiction: Jacoub in the laboratory manufactures a white beast whose evil progeny are rampant in today's world. *Great Goodness of Life* (1969, dedicated 'with love and respect' to Baraka's father) is the expressionist trial of Court Royal, who longs for the great goodness of life as lived by white middle-class America, and who therefore follows the commands of a mysterious Voice. After killing his black nationalist son, he is free to go bowling. *Madheart* (1967) is a morality play in which a black Everyman moves past female obstacles – a white Devil Lady, an Uncle Tom mother, an assimilationist sister, and an independent Black Woman, whom he subdues to his will. In *Jello* (1965), a burlesque of the Jello-sponsored Jack Benny show, the black servant Rochester rises up against his white employers. *Bloodrites* (1970) is a dance drama in which a black chorus exorcise white devils of the mass media, enabling them to raise a black man from the ground.

Slave Ship (1967) is subtitled 'A Historical Pageant'. Subduing his verbal flow, Baraka relies upon music to support his images of black history: the proud native Africans, the chained slaves bound for America, the auction block and family dispersal, the seeds of revolt, modern Christian hypocrisy and African sensibility, and the final chant of Afro-American revolutionary power. Although the pageant ends in a celebration with black audience participation, the head of the time-serving minister is rolled into their midst, and actual performances closed with anti-white chants. Kimberly Benston has described Baraka's dramatic development: 'The tragedy-burdened slave ship of *Dutchman* has become the dance-filled celebration of *Slave Ship*; musical transcendence has risen from the spirit of tragedy.'

In 1974 Baraka renounced black nationalism for international Marxist–Leninist–Maoist thought, and his writing has become didactic. *S–1* and *The Motion of History* (1976) recall left-wing theatre of the 1930s, except that the protagonists are black. *The Motion of History* recapitulates some of the material of *Slave Ship*, but history narrows down to Richie and Lennie, modern 'white and Black dudes', who gradually renounce Bohemia for commitment to workers' revolution. The dramatic energy that drove Baraka's earlier styles has subsided to pulpit didacticism in a very different religion from that of his clergyman forefathers.

Born within a few hundred miles and a few months (in 1934) of one another, Baraka and Ed Bullins entered different worlds – the black bourgeoisie and the black ghetto, respectively. Bullins has said that all the men of his family belong to the criminal class; he was the first to attend high school, but he dropped out. Baraka joined the Air Force in reaction against the university, but Bullins joined the Navy after living from hand to mouth. Yet both young

111

blacks managed to read insatiably during their enlistments. After his military stint, Bullins went back to school, acquiring a high-school diploma. He drifted westward to Los Angeles and enrolled in writing courses at Los Angeles City College, then moved north to San Francisco State University. Like Baraka, Bullins began writing in a variety of genres, including verse, essays and fiction. 'I turned to writing plays because I found that the people I was interested in writing about or writing to – my people – didn't read much fiction, essays, or poetry.' Unsaid is the sad fact that his people do not see many plays either. Bullins and a few friends produced his first plays in the Off-Off-Broadway of San Francisco, where he became for a short time Minister of Culture for the Black Panthers. When Robert Macbeth of Harlem's New Lafayette Theatre sent him a plane ticket, Bullins flew east and made that theatre his home from 1967 to 1972.

Bullins' first plays date from 1965, sometimes dramatising his fiction and usually satirising black bourgeois life, as in the widely anthologised *Electronic Nigger* (1968), with its shocking and self-explanatory title.

In his first year of dramatic writing, Bullins drew upon his familiarity with the black lower depths for *Clara's Ole Man* (1965). In a Philadelphia slum eighteen-year-old Clara has invited Jack of the Ivy League suit and diction to visit her 'in the afternoon when her ole man would be at work'. Jack finds that Clara lives with Baby Girl and Big Girl. Enter three sixteen-year-olds who have robbed an old man; they are quickly subdued by Big Girl. After much wine, Big Girl takes Clara to the show to which Jack has invited her, and the young toughs take Jack outside to beat him up – on the prior order of Big Girl, who is Clara's ole man.

The pieces in *Four Dynamite Plays* (1971) resemble Baraka's revolutionary plays – short, simplistic, filled with anti-white obscenities. *It Bees That Way* (1970) is Bullins' version of *Offending the Audience*, with slum blacks turning upon their white audience. In *Death List* (1970) a black revolutionary lists for execution actual blacks who supported the state of Israel. (The entire collection is dedicated to Al-Fatah.) *Pig Pen* (1970) paints a miscellaneous group of Bohemian blacks, upon whom the assassination of Malcolm X has little effect. *Night of the Beast* (1970) is a film script about a black–white civil war, with victory to the blacks.

In his most telling plays Bullins dramatises the black urban ghetto. He prefaces his first collection with a quotation from Baraka: 'All their faces turned into the lights and you work on them black nigger magic, and cleanse them at having seen the ugliness and if the beautiful sees themselves, they will love themselves.' Bullins' characters are thieves, pimps, prostitutes, drug-pushers, and yet they have spirit and humour. Like Chekhov, Bullins probes the faults of his people to 'cleanse them at having seen the ugliness'.

In the mid-1960s Bullins began work on a cycle of twenty plays about Afro-Americans between 1900 and 1999, but he has continued to write plays outside the cycle too. Perhaps the most cheerily chilling of the latter group is *Goin' a Buffalo* (1968). Like Chekhov's Three Sisters who dream of going to Moscow, Bullins' pimps and whores dream of escaping from Los Angeles to Buffalo: 'I heard that Buffalo is really boss.' Through death and betrayal, the dream approaches reality. One black betrays his friend, annexes his black and white molls, and orders the women to pack. When asked where they are going, he replies, to close the play, 'To Buffalo, baby. Where else?'

Another extra-cycle play was commissioned by Gordon

Davidson for the Mark Taper Forum – *The Taking of Miss Janie* (1975). The play opens with a brutal 'taking of [white] Miss Janie' by rape. An extended flashback reveals how the white woman and black man met at school in the hip scene of the 1960s, where a black nationalist rages against easy integration. One black–white marriage survives in spite of friction; a black woman becomes a lesbian after two marriages (one to the protagonist Monty); another black woman slips easily into anyone's bed; two Jewish men diverge into drug addict and Bahai addict. By the end of the play Monty offers love to Miss Janie, in the form of more sexual pleasure than she has ever known – or so he promises. In spite of its anti-semitism, the play won the 1975 New York Drama Critics Circle Award, but Bullins worried about poor attendance: 'Maybe the whites are threatened and the niggers are embarrassed.'

The plays of Bullins' Afro-American cycle lend each other strength. They are not being written in chronological order, and they are linked not by plot but by characters weaving through separate plays. What seems to be the first chronologically is one of the last to be written, *Home Boy* (1976). Unusual for Bullins is the small-town Southern setting for two young friends, Jody and Dude. The latter soon escapes to a Northern city, where he learns stealing, whoring, dope-dealing, and, in his words, 'revoltin' and revolutionin''.

Although Bullins no longer mentions the one-act *Corner* (1968) as part of his cycle, it offers a first view of Cliff Dawson, one of the cycle's protagonists. Set on a Los Angeles street corner in the 1950s, it sketches young ghetto blacks who spend aimless days drinking, stealing, fornicating. Drunk and desultorily flirting with Cliff's girl Stella, the young blacks taunt one another with sharp wit. When the acknowledged leader Cliff arrives, he parks a drunken

Stella in a broken-down car for a gang rape. He confesses to his friend Bummie that he has impregnated Lou, who has been supporting him: 'You can start callin' me Daddy Cliff.' *In the Wine Time* (1968) shows Cliff's ménage, a perpetual wine time for Cliff and Lou's fifteen-year-old nephew. Cliff lives on pregnant Lou's earnings while he drinks and whores. When nephew Ray stabs another teen-ager, Cliff takes the blame, so that the teenager can avoid prison. *In New England Winter* (1967) finds Cliff after seven years in prison. His half-brother, Steve Benson, mas-terminds a robbery in order to rejoin an old love in New England in winter. The play intercuts 1955 New England scenes with the 1960 robbery rehearsal – a four-man rehearsal demanding disguise and precise timing. Intellec-tual Steve cuts his friend Bummie's throat to prevent the revelation of a Steve–Lou love affair during Cliff's impri-sonment: 'But it was for nothing, Steve ... I knew.' With Bummie dead, three men successfully perform the rob-bery.

The Duplex (1970) houses Steve in Los Angeles during the 1960s. A sometime student, he shares his top-floor flat with Marco Polo Henderson. The first-floor flat is occu-pied by the duplex owner Velma, married to brutal O. D., but loved by Steve, who has apparently not gone to New England. The duplex is the locale of pointless pleasures – cards, wine, marijuana, adultery. The play's subtitle, 'A Black Love Fable in Four Movements', signals Steve's two approaches toward and retreats from Velma. After Steve is nearly killed by Velma's husband, and Velma is clearly victimised by his violence, old Montgo-mery Henderson breezes innocently into the duplex to con-clude the play: 'Hey, ev'va body! Grab yo cards, whiskey 'n'women! It's party time!'

In *The Fabulous Miss Marie* (1970) it is always party

time; that is why Miss Marie (Steve's occasional mistress in the preceding play) is fabulous. Daughter of a university graduate, granddaughter of a schoolteacher, Marie when pregnant married dancer Bill Horton. He brought her to Los Angeles, where he parks cars for 'two hundred stone cold dollars a week. . . . We make almost as much as some colored doctors make . . . 'n we spend it too. 'Cause it's party time every day at Miss Marie's house.' Miss Marie's Christmas-party guests proclaim that they are having a good time, but boredom seeps through the tired language of schoolteacher, social worker, dress-designer. Bullins' black bourgeoisie lack the vigour and invention of his ghetto criminals. Like Chekhov's dying aristocrats, Bullins' anachronistic bourgeois indulge themselves in a world that is passing them by.

Bullins has produced no single play as powerful as Baraka's *Dutchman*, but he is a more consistent dramatic craftsman. Evident both in and outside the cycle are his sharp command of the *humour* of black colloquial speech, an ear attuned to its rhythms, and a lack of inhibition about its lyricism. Baraka and Bullins both seek wide audiences for their plays of Afro-American experience, but for different reasons. Baraka is a convert to Marxist Maoism, whereas Bullins is 'investigating the idea that Marxism is a Zionist conspiracy'. For Baraka, writing is an instrument toward a life-pattern, and his recent plays deal discursively with revolutionary pattern. Bullins, one-time Cultural Minister for the Black Panthers, seems disenchanted with politics and determined to make his writing 'the central activity, the mainstay, the source, the wellspring, the guiding tenet'.

Although Bullins' *Jo Anne* (1976) vindicates a black woman prisoner who killed the white guard who raped her, most of his plays, like those of Baraka, dramatise the new black *male* consciousness. Adrienne Kennedy, in contrast, dramatises her own black and lyrical *un*conscious: 'I see my writing as being an outlet for inner, psychological confusion and questions stemming from childhood.... You try to struggle with the material that is lodged in your unconscious, and try to bring it to the conscious level.'

In early background, Kennedy is closer to Baraka than to Bullins. Born in 1931 in Pittsburgh into a middle-class black family, she was brought up in a mixed neighbourhood in Cleveland. Like Baraka, she went to university and found most of her studies irrelevant to her life. Like Baraka, too, she was drawn to the avant-garde of New York City in the early 1960s, but her plays differ from any of his styles. Describing her plays as 'states of mind', she does herself theatrical injustice. Her plays are *acts* of mind – tremulous or masterful, but always eloquent, with powerful images.

While far from New York she wrote *Funnyhouse of a Negro* (1962) which is set in that city. Often cited as her best work, this drama announces her main style, sometimes called surrealist and sometimes expressionist, and actually a delicate blend of aspects of both. Kennedy's plays are expressionist in their subjectivity, with inner conflicts externalised as different characters; they are surrealist in their close dependence on dreams with strong visual images. They are original in the particular images and in the incantatory repetitions that extend the subjective into the mythic.

The 'funnyhouse' of *Funnyhouse of a Negro* is both setting and metaphor for the dwelling of negro Sarah. The play's characters are divided into white and coloured, but the division shifts subtly. Sarah is the titular negro, whose 'funnyhouse' is dominated by a white landlady and a Jewish lover. Sarah's light-skinned mother looks white, and Sarah herself is the product of her black father's rape of her

117

mother. Torn between the two strands of her heritage, Sarah is seen and heard through four selves – white Queen Victoria and Duchess of Hapsburg, black Patrice Lumumba, and yellow hunchbacked Jesus. Through the speech of all four selves runs the motif of her black father, whose search for identity is transmitted to his daughter. A dark man, he disappoints his mother by marrying Sarah's light mother, whom he then drives mad by taking her to Africa to engage in missionary work. His black spirit duels with his yellow-skinned daughter, who is haunted by his suicide after the murder of Lumumba. When Sarah's several selves fragment and repeat one another, '*her father's black figures with bludgeoned hands rush upon her, the lights black and we see her hanging in the room*'. The white landlady repeats Sarah's account of her father's Harlem hanging after Lumumba's murder, but the white poet ends the play in denial: 'Her father is a nigger who eats his meals on a white glass table.' There is neither truth nor rest for the perturbed spirits in the white funnyhouse of a negro.

This summary arranges Kennedy's scenes into a rationality that is poetically denied by her visual and verbal imagination. In the opening mime, for example, a wild-haired woman in white mask and nightgown walks dreaming across the stage, carrying a bald head. The Queen and Duchess wear identical cheap white gowns and headpieces from which frizzy hair shows, and they talk about their dead black father, who keeps returning to the house. The negro Sarah is dressed in black, with a rope around her neck, and she is frightened by her lack of self-awareness. Kennedy's funnyhouse figures change shape, distortedly mirroring one another. As Patrice Lumumba, Sarah half-repeats what she said as the negro: 'My friends will be white. I need them as an embankment to keep me from reflecting too much upon the fact that I am Patrice Lumumba who haunted my mother's conception.' Throughout the play Kennedy bases striking scenes on hair – baldness, wild straight hair, frizzy hair, hair torn out in patches, a nimbus on African heads. A traditional fertility symbol becomes a torture chamber. The play circles back to its beginning, with a black man knocking at the door and a negro woman hanging in her funnyhouse.

The Owl Answers (1963) continues the distinctive expressionist/surrealist idiom forged by Kennedy. Again the woman protagonist has several *alter egos*, formulaically repeated: 'She who is Clara Passmore, who is the Virgin Mary who is the Bastard who is the Owl.' Set in the subway, like *Dutchman*, the play also reaches for myth. The subway is 'the Tower of London is a Harlem Hotel Room is St Peter's', and from scene to scene the whole set moves to show these facets. Other than the protagonist, a black mother and white father shift identities as they '*change slowly back and forth into and out of themselves*'. As Sarah of *Funnyhouse* is torn between English culture and the split strands of her black heritage, so the protagonist, She, is fragmented between Clara Passmore, the Virgin, a Bastard and an Owl, but also between her black mother and the English literary tradition of her white Southern ancestor. She is imprisoned in the Tower of London by William the Conqueror, Anne Boleyn and Shakespeare; at a violent moment she hears the third movement of Haydn's Horn Concerto in D.

She is not only a black woman seeking her identity in a father or the father-substitutes she lures to Harlem hotel rooms; she is also a writer who writes to her father every day, and who drops notebook pages throughout the alogical, highly imaged action. She is at once the bastard of a rich white man and his black cook, and the schoolteacher daughter of a coloured clergyman and his wife. Shunted between Harlem and London (in circular turns of the stage subway), she knows no rest: 'I call God and the Owl answers.' In prayer, her mother stabs herself, and on the altar she tries to stab the negro who desires her. At the last 'She who is Clara who is The Bastard who is The Virgin Mary suddenly looks like an owl, and lifts her bowed head, stares into space and speaks: "Ow . . . owww."' Bird of traditional wisdom, Kennedy's owl cries the question 'Whoooo?' and answers in pain 'Ow . . . oww.'

Paired with *The Owl Answers* as *Cities in Bezique* (a card game coupling Queen of Spades and Jack of Diamonds), *A Beast Story* (1969) continues Kennedy's animal imagery and her fusion of expressionism and surrealism. Explicitly, the scenic directions inform us that the beasts – mother, father, and daughter – are a black minister's family, isolated from one another in stage rooms.

The beast is a rat in *A Rat's Mass* (1966), where rathood is a metaphor for blackness. Brother and Sister Rat are both in love with white Italian Rosemary, who wears a confirmation dress but has worms in her hair. As She of *The Owl Answers* is drawn to literary London, so Brother and Sister Rat are drawn to Italian Catholicism in a time of Nazi armies. When the rat siblings intone phrases of a Rosemary who has refused to atone them, shots destroy them, and only Rosemary of the worm-hair remains.

Animal imagery is more subdued in *A Lesson in Dead Language* (1968). The scene is an ordinary classroom, except that the teacher is a white dog *'from the waist up'*. To seven little girls dressed in white she teaches a lesson in lyrical language – about bleeding that began when a white dog died. Interspersing the death of Christ, of Caesar and of the sun, Kennedy dramatises menstruation as a rite of admission to a classico-Christian culture. Her own favourite among her plays abjures dream images for this non-realistic classroom where the dog teacher, the larger-than-life Roman and Christian statues, and especially the spreading red stains on white organdie are theatrical symbols of the transition from childhood to womanhood.

Like Baraka and Bullins, Kennedy has written about the murder of Malcolm X, but her play–poem *Sun* (1969) does not even mention his name. A man is in intricate interaction with differently coloured suns and moons. He is slowly dismembered as they bleed and change colour. For all the fragmentation, however, he is sensitive to cosmic rhythms, and, although he is invisible at the last, his voice enunciates his vision through a small black sun.

Kennedy's *Evening with Dead Essex* (1973) is unwontedly realistic. Based on the assassination of black sniper Mark James Essex, and dedicated to him and his family, the play resorts to a play within the play, but Kennedy stipulates, 'The actors use their real names and the director should get the actors to play themselves.' Black actors soberly enact the life and death of Essex. Only the Projectionist is white, suggesting the surface view of a white world that murdered this idealistic young black from the Mid-West. Through the actors' rehearsal, we piece together the story of an idealist whose disillusion turns to murder of racists. Understanding Essex, the black actors look at the projection of films and close their play with phrases from the Gospel of Luke: 'To heal the brokenhearted'.

Kennedy's *Movie Star Has to Star in Black and White* was directed by Joe Chaikin at Joe Papp's Public Theatre in 1976. Resurrecting Clara of *The Owl Answers*, Kennedy embeds her in a different white culture – no longer English literature but American film. Leading roles are played by Bette Davis, Paul Henreid, Jean Peters, Marlon Brando, Montgomery Clift, and Shelley Winters. The male actors do not speak, and Clara speaks through the several women. Supporting roles go to the expressionistically conceived Mother, Father, Husband.

A prologue introduces the seamless shifts from Clara the writer to Clara the daughter of the Mother and Father, the pregnant wife of Eddie, the mother of Eddie Junior, and the *alter ego* of white film actresses: 'Each day I wonder with what or with whom can I co-exist in a true union?'

Set on the ocean liner from *Now Voyager*, the first scene reveals the conflict between Clara's light mother and dark father, as well as the strains between Clara and her husband. The second scene merges *Viva Zapata* with a hospital in which Clara's brother Wally lies in a coma after an automobile accident. Through the figure of Jean Peters, Clara thinks back to *The Owl Answers* and forward to the play that she hopes to write. The third scene brings a small rowing-boat to the stage, with Shelley Winters and Montgomery Clift as they appear in *A Place in the Sun*. Jean Peters and Marlon Brando keep changing the sheets of a bleeding Clara, who keeps writing. Her husband Eddie charges 'that my diaries consume me and that my diaries make me a spectator watching my life like watching a black and white movie'. When Montgomery Clift impassively watches Shelley Winters drown, we hear that Clara's brother Wally will live with a damaged brain. Family tragedy merges with fictional tragedy for playwright and play.

Kennedy has set a mystery novel, *Deadly Triplets* (1989), in her world of theatre – London's Royal Court and New York's Off-Broadway. Under the mystery-evoking title *The Ohio State Murders* (1990) Kennedy has dramatised insidious white violence against a sensitive black woman. A playwright who never forces her talent, Adrienne Kennedy has absorbed expressionist subjectivism and surrealist dream imagery to sound her own unique timbre. Intensely personal, her plays are contemporary renderings of the myth of the double. At the same time, they dramatise a black woman's experience in a dominant white male culture.

Colour-blind casting is still a rarity in the last decade of the twentieth century, but the achievements of these four black playwrights may have facilitated production for the next generation. Like Ed Bullins before him, August Wilson (b. 1945) plans a cycle of plays about the history of black Americans. The springboard for each play is the blues, so it is not surprising that Wilson begins with *Ma Rainey's Black Bottom* (1985), a tough and talented portrait of a tough and immensely talented black singer. Music also drives the self-styled 'choreopoems' of Ntozake Shange (b. 1948). Originating in 1974 performances in the bars of San Francisco, her *for colored girls who have considered suicide / when the rainbow is enuf* was an undiluted Broadway success by 1976. Wilson has now collaborated with director Lloyd Richards to bring four plays to New York – loosely plotted and realistic, except for the music. Shange has had five plays produced, ranging from her choreopoems to an adapted *Mother Courage*. Each of these playwrights focuses on different aspects of black American experience, and both seem impervious to the blandishments of prizes and promises. However, those prizes – so rarely awarded their seniors – carry new promise for theatre in the United States. A rainbow coalition in culture keeps pace with a black mayor in New York City and a black governor in Virginia.

8
From Gay to Ridiculous: Duberman, Patrick, Tavel, Bernard, Ludlam

The first anthology of gay plays, published only in 1979, classifies as gay any play 'whose central figure or figures are homosexual or one in which homosexuality is a main theme'. Editor William Hoffman pinpoints Mae West's *Drag* (1927) as the first American homosexual play. In *Drag*, as well as her *Pleasure Man* (1928) Hoffman hears a plea for sexual tolerance. I hear that plea also in Lillian Hellman's *Children's Hour* (1934), but Hoffman finds that she treats homosexuality 'with little lucidity'.

Given the paucity of gay plays, some critics have dredged homosexuality from the depths of 'straight' plays, notably those of Tennessee Williams and Edward Albee. For example, Georges-Michel Sarotte in *Like a Brother, Like a Lover* states unequivocally, 'our supposition [is] that Williams never treats heterosexuality without embodying himself in the heroine', and 'Between *The Zoo Story* and *Who's Afraid of Virginia Woolf?* Albee wrote *The Sandbox*, *The American Dream*, and *The Death of Bessie Smith*. These three plays are also of assistance in confirming the basic

124

homosexuality of Albee's work.' Such cheap psychoanaly-
sis denies that these dramatists are superbly capable of
choosing their own subjects and dramatising them to
attract audiences of all sexual persuasions.

Ignoring the sex life of playwrights, which I anachronisti-
cally believe to be their own affair, I devote this chapter
to plays that dramatise not only homosexual but also cross-
sexual and androgynous figures. Not until the 1960s, following the lead of blacks who addressed drama to their
colleagues, did homosexual playwrights come out of the
proverbial closet. It is surely by design that white homosexual historian Martin Duberman wrote his first play about
the black plight 'In White America', but analogous protests
about life 'in male America' are rare before the AIDS plague
in the 1980s, since gay playwrights tend more to literal
gayness than protest.

The *OED Supplement* yields no clues as to how 'gay'
came to mean homosexual, but it quotes examples from
the 1950s. Duberman himself veers from the sober docu-
mentation of *In White America* to the witticisms of his
gay plays, and Robert Patrick shares this witty vein.
Charles Ludlam, Ronald Tavel and Kenneth Bernard call
their plays 'ridiculous', which seems like a companionable
adjective for 'gay'. The gay characters of these male playwrights are usually male.

Martin Duberman, born in New York City in 1930 and
educated to doctoral level at Ivy League schools, is a historian who has also written plays. The theme of his single
collection is gayness. Its title, *Male Armor* (1968 and 1974),
is based upon Wilhelm Reich's 'character armour' or 'the
devices we use (which then use us) to protect ourselves
from our own energy, and especially from our sexual
energy'. What Duberman calls 'evasive sparring partners'
dominate a number of the plays – *Metaphors, The*

Recorder, *The Electric Map*. Evasive though the partners may be to one another, they are quite transparent to an audience who can see through the armour to a homosexual 'pass'. In *Metaphors* a Yale University interviewer is accosted by a bright, unconventional applicant for university admission. In *Colonial Dudes* a professor and student grow progressively open to one another's language. In *The Recorder* an oral historian, armed with recorder, tries to listen in on the intimate life of the long-time companion of a deceased public figure. In *The Electric Map* two brothers, natives of history-drenched Gettysburg, respectively blame and defend their mother for the homosexuality of one of them; Duberman tries to weave the failure of the old family into the failure of the old South. *The Guttman Ordinary Scale* is a broad satire on 'scientific' sexual testing.

Of the seven plays in Duberman's collection only two are extended dramas, and, for that reason perhaps, they have not been produced in an Off-Off-Broadway that prefers shorter, looser and less comprehensive fare. *Payments* (1971) revolves around the fragile marriage of Nancy and Bob – fragile because Bob needs to break out of marriage periodically, into sex and alcohol binges. Happening to meet Sal, an old school friend who manages a call-boy service, Nancy offers him her husband's services, with a view toward obtaining financial and sexual 'payments' toward their faltering marriage. Her scheme fails, but we become spectators (voyeurs?) of Bob's initiation into the male homosexual world of New York City – witty transvestites, affluent executive, cynical journalist, brutal Marine. Each homosexual is a sociological type, and the central couple is a suburban case history; in spite of wit, violence and costume change, the drama lacks drama.

Elagabalus (1973) is named after the third-century

Roman emperor, who also fascinated Artaud. Manipulating and manipulated by mother and grandmother, Elagabalus shocked Rome by his sensual self-indulgence, elevating homosexual commoners to positions of power. Duberman creates contemporary New Yorker Adrian Donner, a strikingly beautiful and wealthy young man, who poses as the Emperor Elagabalus, and leads a similar life of sensual self-indulgence. Despite his grandmother's objections, he begins a lavish marriage ceremony with two brides at once – his middle-aged Puerto Rican cleaning-woman and his young stable-boy lover. 'The results will be everything you wish. The process everything I wish.' Process and results coincide when Adrian stabs himself to death, after which his recorded voice narrates the death of Roman Emperor Elagabalus. Adrian's faithful Puerto Rican servant places a ring on his inert finger, while his recorded voice hails the promise of a life of pleasure. The contemporary character, like his Roman model, died because the world was not yet ready for a life devoted to sensual pleasure.

Although Duberman's plays have met with little appreciation, he is emblematic of an American trend of the 1960s. In the radical year 1968 he strayed from history, his vocation, into drama, an avocation, using his considerable intellect and learning to decry intellect and learning: ingredients of 'male armour'. Even more anti-intellectual and anti-rational is his *Visions of Jack Kerouac* (1976), which Duberman himself describes as 'a meditation on Kerouac's life'. The play is preceded by a quotation from Allen Ginsberg's introduction to Kerouac's *Visions of Cody*, which wishes that the two friends had been 'physically tenderer' to one another. Duberman rambles through the early days of the Beats at Columbia University, their subsequent raucous encounters, their cultivation of sensual derangement, their experiments with spontaneous writing ('Craft is crafty'), their pansexuality but Kerouac's horror of homosexuality. The implication is that Kerouac's vestigial Puritanism about homosexuality caused his disintegration through alcohol and a mother fixation.

Robert Patrick, born in Texas in 1937, has published this thumbnail autobiography:

His childhood was spent ostensibly in many different Depression states but actually he grew up in the worldwide media mesh of slick-paper magazines, radio serials, paperback pocket books and above all the slowly expanding screens of all-powerful Hollywood. This led him to New York, where, in 1961, he followed a Salvation Army Band to the Caffe Cino. He more or less lived there until it closed in 1968, proceeding to become, meanwhile, Off-Off-Broadway's most-produced playwright.

Emblematic is the sequence of education in the mass media (rather than school) and drift to Off-Off-Broadway. Unmentioned is the homosexuality that made Patrick *persona grata* at Caffe Cino. A self-educated actor–director–designer–technician before he became a playwright, Patrick has written over 150 plays and published four collections of them. Many of them dramatise homosexuality – literally gay with a surface of glib patter.

Patrick's first 'Cheap Theatrick', *The Haunted Host* (1964), features a homosexual playwright haunted by the ghost of his lover. Enter a young lookalike of the dead lover, new to Greenwich Village and its gay scene. Most of the play consists of dialogue between 'depraved queers and simple country boys', the country boy feeding lines to the whipping wit of the depraved queer (played originally by Harvey Fierstein). A declaration of love exorcises the host's ghost.

One Person (1969) is again set on the gay scene of New York City. An actor's *tour de force*, it may be influenced by Lanford Wilson's *Madness of Lady Bright*. The obsessive speaker is not, however, a drag queen, but a male homosexual. The 'one person' plays to invisible characters, and the play's title threads through the addresses of the speaker to his lover: 'I was one person, and you were one person, and then we – we were one person. . .'. When the homosexual lovers – provisionally 'one person' – emerge into the gay-bar scene, the lover goes off with someone else: 'When you see two people, walking that close together, and walking away that fast, they look – at first – like one person.'

T-Shirts (1978) is also set on the New York gay scene. The play's three characters are a decade apart in age: forty-year-old Marvin, a playwright who loves to travel; his apartment-mate Kink, a thirty-year-old interior decorator; and handsome twenty-year-old Tom, who seeks shelter in their flat on a rainy night. Tom proves to be a hustler: 'Older guys have the connections and – okay – the money, and, hell, you can learn a lot from older guys.' While Tom changes into a dry T-shirt and shorts, the older men query one another's intentions. Disgusted with Tom's preening, Kink leaves to pick someone up at the baths, and Marvin departs for Rome, a pocketful of T-shirts his only luggage.

Although editor William Hoffman reads *T-Shirts* as a 'crash-course in what it's like to be a sophisticated gay man', it is a crash-course in what it's like to be prey to camp *bon mots*. The stage T-shirts are stamped with tired epigrams; the two older men lapse into tired comic routines; but young Tom proves more shopworn and cynical than they. Between 1964 and 1978 Patrick's handsome young stranger changed from the country boy of *Haunted Host* to the depraved hustler of *T-Shirts*, but his sophisticated gay playwright brandishes the same wicked wit in a flimsy dramatic structure. And this is true, too, of his *Untold Decades: Seven Comedies of Gay Romance* (1988), even to the final monologue of an AIDS-infected queen of the 1980s.

Patrick's numerous plays treat a range of subjects in a variety of styles, but his best-known work remains *Kennedy's Children* (1973). Its five characters speak in monologues. Patrick's scenic directions specify: '*At no time do the characters relate to one another, not even at their moments of greatest duress.*'

'Kennedy's children' number five, three women and two men, musing in a Lower East Side bar of New York City, like O'Neill's denizens of Harry Hope's Bar. Patrick's people are stock types of the 1960s; both men are homosexual (or bisexual) – a soldier back from Vietnam and an Off-Off-Broadway actor. One woman is a would-be sex symbol, another a former political activist, and a third has been traumatised by Kennedy's assassination with its concomitant assassination of faith in those who are 'bigger and better than other people'. Five portraits of progressive disenchantment, the monologues dovetail only in occasional references to drugs, blacks, and the mass media – those key symbols of the 1960s. Of particular relish for theatre *aficionados* is the actor's recollection of Off-Off Broadway:

At eight o'clock, I was the left thumb in a group sensitivity demonstration called 'Hands Off' in Merrymount Episcopal Community Center, and then at ten I played a movie projector with a twinkle bulb in my mouth in a drag production of 'Bonnie and Clyde' at the Mass Dramatists Experimental Tavern, and at the stroke of midnight, I was the cathectic focus of a rather tedious telepathic theatre event in the basement of the Yoga Institute. That one wasn't advertised. We all just sat together and tried to draw Clive Barnes to us with the power of prayer. I try to keep busy.

'That', as Albee's Jerry says in another context, 'is the jazz of a very special hotel', and Patrick's play aims at a larger theme – the waste of Kennedy's children without a Kennedy. A facile way of conveying fragmentation, the five monologues are mood pieces about nostalgia for heroes, but they do not probe the ideal of the leader. *Kennedy's Children* profits from the casual integration of gays into the social fabric of the 1960s, a period when heroes 'died or were killed . . . sold out or ran away' – like most periods.

Critic Stefan Brecht calls Off-Off-Broadway homosexuality 'Queer Theatre', but the major practitioners – John Vaccaro, Ronald Tavel, Charles Ludlam – prefer the adjective 'ridiculous'. Director John Vaccaro and author Ronald Tavel dispute the honour of first attributing that adjective to their theatres. Whoever is right, the original Playhouse of the Ridiculous performed Tavel's manic word-plays under Vaccaro's manic direction. Foreseeably, the two explosive personalities parted company – in 1967, when Vaccaro, excising chunks of Tavel's *Gorilla Queen*, evidently cut him to the quick. Tavel moved his play to the Judson Poets' Theatre, and Vaccaro substituted a play by Ridiculous actor Charles Ludlam. The Vaccaro–Ludlam partnership lasted less than a year. In 1967 Vaccaro staged *Conquest of the Universe* by a dissatisfied Ludlam, who thereupon withdrew to found the Ridiculous Theatrical Company. Fortuitously, Kenneth Bernard offered his plays to Vaccaro, who then directed seven Bernard plays between 1967 and 1979. Ludlam has stated that his theatre is an actor's theatre, Tavel's a playwright's theatre and Vaccaro's a director's theatre, but these distinctions are not evident in performance.

Native New Yorkers – Bernard born in 1930, Tavel in 1941, and Ludlam in 1943 – all three are city sophisticates. Ludlam is a BA in dramatic art, Tavel an MA in philosophy and literature, and Bernard a PhD in language and literature. Yet the three were nurtured on popular arts, which are reflected in their drama.

In 1966 Tavel wrote in *TriQuarterly*, 'Theatre of the Ridiculous is a community of Ourselves taking momentary time to laugh at its position as the ridiculous.' He names the main influences as pop, camp, psychedelic and art nouveau, but he does not mention the gay ambience. Tavel has written over thirty plays, as well as a novel, essays, films and verse. Distinguishing his early from his later work he has written, 'In the early plays I . . . attempted to destroy plot and character, motivation, cause, event, and logic along with their supposed consequences. The word was all. . . . The full-length plays after *Gorilla Queen* obey, I believe [Aristotle's] difficult insights.' Although Tavel wrote plays when he was still in his teens, he gained notoriety through his film scenarios for Andy Warhol (1964–6). When Warhol rejected Tavel's *Shower* (1965), it was staged live by John Vaccaro. And thus the Playhouse of the Ridiculous was born, already bearing its family features – disjointed episodes rather than plot, shifting character identities, burlesque of and affection for popular genres, obscene word-play, hints of Pirandellianism or play-within-play.

During the next two years Tavel wrote other short plays in swift succession – *Vinyl*, *Kitchenette*, *The Life of Juanita Castro* and *The Life of Lady Godiva*, which were not produced in the order written. *Lady Godiva* is perhaps the most popular of this group. Originally played by a man, the lady rides on an elongated horse equipped with steering-wheel, rear-view mirror, brake, accelerator; this contraption is driven by Peeping Tom (played by Charles Ludlam). The lady seeks new soles in Coventry Convent, where a corps of transvestite nuns are ruled by Mother Superviva (played by Vaccaro): 'Nudity is the quintessence of essence, though it is sickrilegious to say so.' After sexual fun and games, 'Lady Godiva rides nude at high noon' on Mother Superviva, but Sister Kasha Veronicas cobbles the soles and shoes the naked lady.

Tavel produced a few plays in order to fill out an evening in the theatre. When *Shower* lasted only an hour, Tavel composed *The Life of Juanita Castro*, which 'should never be rehearsed' since its form is a rehearsal – for a film. (It was filmed by Warhol.) The director and Juanita are played by men, while Fidel, Raul and Che are played by women.

Indira Gandhi's Daring Device (1966), a 'smellodrama', was again too short for a full evening, so Tavel wrote *Screen Test*, which soon usurped most of the evening because of actor Ludlam's irrepressible improvisations. As in *Juanita Castro*, a director rehearses for a film; his two actresses are a woman and a transvestite (originally played by Mario Montez, who himself burlesqued 1940s actress Maria Montez). In performance the woman did not attain the panache of the transvestite, who perfectly rendered feminine sexuality as synthesised by Hollywood. A second transvestite then competed with the first – actor Charles Ludlam as Norma Desmond, an aging Hollywood star aching for a comeback, who is instead kidnapped by a gorilla.

In 1967 the gorilla-actor, Harvey Tavel, became the director of his brother's *Kitchenette*, which burlesques domestic comedy through a film rehearsal. In a littered kitchenette (replete with improbable toilet) Harvey Tavel directed two couples, female Jo and male Mikie, male Joe and female Mickey: 'Well, why the hell does everybody around here have to have the same name? How am I supposed to know who to have sex with?' After crosscouplings, Jo stabs Mikie with a marshmallow fork and is in turn strangled on a mattress, as the remaining three actors intone, 'Matric-ide on a mattress!'

Moving to longer plays, Tavel wrote *Gorilla Queen* (1967), which he sees as the first of his Aristotelian dramas. Enlarging the role of the gorilla of *Screen Test*, this ambitious play became the occasion of Tavel's declaration of independence from director John Vaccaro, who demanded abridgements. Tavel moved it intact to the Judson Memorial Church, where it was directed by Living Theatre veteran Lawrence Kornfeld. Set in a Hollywood jungle, *Gorilla Queen* casts transsexual Queen Kong as the object of Clyde Batty's quest. Tavel considers his play to have a linear Aristotelian plot, but it is hard to extract beginning, middle and end from these movie scenes in a mix-master, where a White Woman and Sister Carries are played by men. Clyde shoots Kong and somehow becomes him/her through a Deus Sex Mattachine.

In his next few plays Tavel caricatures contemporary America less affectionately. *Arenas of Lutetia* (1968) combines Greek and Christian myths through the brothers Actaeon and Sebastian. The latter is the author of *Arenas of Lutetia* – the Piran-Tavel twist – and the arenas are a jungle of creation presided over by muse Lutetia in a *lingua franca* of sexual puns that mock Bohemian America and Hollywood epics. Inhabitually economical is Tavel's next play, which is sometimes considered his best. *Boy on the Straight-Back Chair* (1969) is frighteningly heterosexual (as implied in the title's 'straight') in dramatising 'our town's dirty laundry' or seduction–murders by Toby Short. Based on actual murders committed by Charles Schmid, the play also draws upon other 'pleasure' killers in the violent society of contemporary America. Subduing his invention, Tavel renounces the ridiculous in this grim drama of the humourless playboy of the American West.

After several contemporary satires, Tavel produced his favourite play, *Bigfoot* (1970). The play's title refers to the Abominable Snowman, and the play itself recycles the old Romantic theme of divided brothers – Esau and Jacob (who becomes Jack), Alpha and Omega, and finally, Ronald Tavel's actual brother Harvey, who arranges Jack's departure through the audience. Having scorned the intellect in essay and burlesque, Tavel surprisingly wrote this turgid and undramatic debate, with long metaphysical speeches supplanting action.

Although Tavel continued to write (if not to publish) in the 1980s – *The Understudy* (1981), *Success and Succession* (1983), *Notorious Harik Will Kill the Pope* (1986) – I prefer to summarise *Ovens of Anita Orangejuice: A History of Modern Florida* (revised 1978). Based on the crusade of Anita Bryant, the play traces her evangelistic struggle for the repeal of the gay rights law. Inconsistently, Tavel gradually enlarges her from caricature to character, mouthing her slogan 'Kill a queer for Christ.' Tavel curbs his verbal pyrotechnics, but he burlesques stock types in a huge cast. The only wholly sympathetic character is a Cuban refugee homosexual, Los Olvidados, who is lynched by the mob inflamed by Anita. Her main weapon is the telephone, and during the course of the play telephone booths become imprisoning boxes, which in turn become crematoria – the titular ovens of Anita Orangejuice. Having effected a holocaust, Anita ends alone on stage, as far as possible from a ringing telephone, and she closes the play, 'Who is calling?' Tied to her telephone, she has no understanding of communication. It is a curiously sympathetic ending for one who has fanned a holocaust. In actual fact, the Florida Citrus Commission terminated Anita Bryant's contract after twelve years; it would be wishful thinking to credit Tavel for that.

Tavel's transsexual exuberance and linguistic games are muted in his plays of the 1970s and 1980s. The uncommitted ridicule of the earlier plays seems definitively behind him, displaced by linear but clumsy plots and ponderous undramatic monologues.

A family man with an academic position, Kenneth Bernard is an unlikely Ridiculous playwright, and he objects to inclusion in this chapter. For him (as for me) 'gay' and 'ridiculous' are not synonyms. Nevertheless, American gay theatre first came to public attention in the context of the Ridiculous, and Bernard's first productions were part of the milieu. Of his work he has written,

> I would hope the appeal of my plays is initially to the emotions only, not the head, and that they are received as spectacle and a kind of gorgeous (albeit frightening) entertainment. The characters in my plays can often be played by either men or women.

In John Vaccaro's direction, the protagonists were sometimes played by transvestites, sometimes by hermaphrodites, sometimes doubled as men and women. In contrast to Ludlam's grotesque sex on stage, to Tavel's transsexual panache, the sexual ambiguity in Bernard's plays is at once magnetic and minatory.

Bernard's first produced play, *The Moke-Eater* (1968), initiated his partnership with Vaccaro, which lasted over a decade. Vaccaro, captivated by *The Moke-Eater* at the very time that Ludlam and his actors left the Playhouse of the Ridiculous, directed it in a restaurant, since greedy and grotesque eating is a repetitive activity in the play. Exposing 'our town's dirty laundry' differently from Tavel, *The Moke-Eater* still preserves plot and character. A contemporary Willy Loman drives into a small town to have his car repaired. The mechanic calls him Fred although he claims to be Jack, and, faced with moronic mumbling of a crowd, he resorts to pidgin English: 'Car no good, Car go click-click. Car bad. Me want fix car. Me pay. (*He waves the money*.) You understandee 'melican boy? Chop-chop?' As the villagers repeat 'Click-click', a dapper leader emerges from their midst: 'Hello, there. I'm Alec. (*He pauses*.) *Smart* Alec.' And smart he proves to be – much smarter than Jack, whom he subjects to a series of humiliations as his only way to escape from the town's stranglehold. Jack is forced to play an animated cartoon, the negro comics Amos and Andy, an appreciator of the American landscape, a song-and-dance man, a formal dinner guest; he is subjected to sexual titillation. Starved while others gorge themselves, tantalised sexually and politically with a promise of release, prevented from urinating, Jack is finally reduced to incoherent crying before '*an amorphous form*' – the moke-eater – devours an old man. Three hours after Jack escapes from the town, he finds himself back there, with everyone frozen in their positions of the play's opening. Only in production did *The Moke-Eater* show the marks of the Ridiculous – in transsexual adornments of furs and feathers, in occasional sallies of demonic laughter, in a female Alec who directs the victimisation of Jack for his and our delectation.

Bubi, the Master of Ceremonies in Bernard's next play, his often-performed *Night Club* (1970), is 'strikingly made up as a woman, but dressed in a tuxedo'. Although his/her sex is indeterminate, the sexuality is 'clear and strong'. In Vaccaro's production the role was doubly played by a veteran Ridiculous actress, Mary Waranow, and a well-known transvestite, Ondine, both of whom were infused with Vaccaro's own demonic, often sadistic energy. The titular night club is Bubi's Hide-Away, where the performers are drawn from an onstage audience who chant Bubi's name as though he were a saviour. And he may be, given the mysterious threatening sounds from the world beyond the night club. Bubi is a cruel master, demanding humiliations like his predecessor Alec, and finally he inveigles the cast to its own 'paradise now' in mass copulation – to the theme music of the Lone Ranger. The one resister is guillotined, and his severed head croaks Bubi's name repeatedly, until he is drowned out by bulldozers and jack-hammers, which in turn are drowned out by the sound of wings flapping high in the sky.

The Magic Show of Dr Ma-Gico (1973) adheres to the same format of master of ceremonies governing performance numbers: 'I do *not* deal in tricks. . . . I deal in life. . . . True magic is metaphor.' This time the setting is not a night club but a seventeenth-century aristocratic drawing-room backed by mirrors, with a throne at the centre and the audience on three sides. Each of the numbers climaxes in violence – a clumsy king knifed in the belly, a young commoner hanged, Esmeralda smothered by gypsies, a young lover castrated during fellatio, a prince killing a king by error, a queen literally loved to death. After knave, courtier and nobleman fail to kill a king, Dr Ma-Gico himself slits his throat. Elegant dances punctuate the numbers in the demonic magic show.

The Sixty-Minute Queer Show (1977) joins Ma-Gico's powerless kings to the drag queens of the Ridiculous.

Although Bernard has written (in a letter to me) that *The Sixty-Minute Queer Show* is 'not particularly about queers', he nevertheless highlights homosexuality by punctuating his vaudeville turns with drag queens – no fewer than ten in his script but reduced to three in Vaccaro's production. Become a composite portrait, the Drag Queen, that most ostentatious of queers, parallels the director figure of Bernard's earlier plays. Hard-edged, double-sexed, prismatic, the Drag Queen manipulates his/her audience as the director manipulates his actors, and he/she does so with skill and style – literally a variety show. In *The Sixty-Minute Queer Show* the drag queens of the interludes are distorted echoes of nominal queens within the scenes, who oppose the order of kings. Two recurrent Bernard types blend in *The Sixty-Minute Queer Show* – ruling figures of a political world and artist figures of an aesthetic world, perhaps mutually exclusive. The 'acts' of the queer show not only pilfer characters and situations from our cultural detritus – king and commoner, lascivious queen and Don Juan lover, trial of a king, Cleopatra and a cowboy lover – but also echo Bernard's own earlier plays, with a new master/mistress of ceremonies in the Drag Queen.

Although Bernard, like Tavel and Ludlam before him, quarrelled with Vaccaro for cutting the script, they became reconciled for two more Bernard productions – *La Justice* (1979) and *La Fin du cirque* (1982) – before the director departed to live in Italy. The very title of *La Justice* (which won a long-overdue Obie) implies a mordant view of that abstraction, whereas *La Fin du cirque* is perhaps Bernard's most insistent juxtaposition of several roles in a single reality. This play, dramatising a European circus fallen on hard times, lacks a controlling androgynous master of ceremonies, but it is framed by the frustrated sexual conjunction of a dwarf and a fat lady in drag. Before their last scene, we witness a grand parade of all the anarchically vulnerable circus company – owner, injured performers, and freaks.

Night club, magic show, queer show, circus and (in *The Panel*, 1984) television – Bernard is relentless in his dramatisation of the spectacular, even as he exposes its cruelties. Although the programme of *The Sixty-Minute Queer Show* offered several definitions of 'queer', and although Stefan Brecht's book *Queer Theatre* reaches out for a virtual metaphysics of the queer, its homosexual centre must not be ignored. Built into Bernard's theatricalisation of a crumbling civilisation is the panache of complexities of gender. He shares the panache with Tavel and Ludlam, but he alone stages the complexities. Central to his drama is the transsexual role of artist/master of magic. Far from catharsis, he/she arouses fear and desire, slaking them only slightly as the show screams on.

Of the three playwrights of the Ridiculous, Charles Ludlam alone has been the subject of a *New Yorker* profile and has had all his plays published. The introduction to the volume that collects all twenty-nine of his plays compares him to Molière. Ludlam's signal achievement was to hold together – sometimes with Scotch tape and rubber bands – a theatre company dedicated to his plays, which are nineteenth-century in spirit (vehicles for Ludlam himself as actor–manager) and late-twentieth-century in free-swinging burlesque, obscenity, sexuality. In Ludlam's own view, he moved from the epic (by which he apparently meant episodic) to the well-made play. *Turds in Hell* (1969, in collaboration with actor Bill Vehr) represents the first technique, and the more popular *Bluebeard* (1970) the second.

The infernal episodes of *Turds in Hell* are played for sexual exuberance rather than intelligible sequence. Turzahnelle abandons her newborn son Orgone on a mountain-top, where he is found by Carla. A large cast of infernal sinners is gathered by Baron Bubbles, a Brazilian Brassiere Buster, who shits money. Romances ensue between the Baron and Turzahnelle, Orgone and nun Vera (Orgone: 'I'm trisexual. I'll try anything'). A St Obnoxious is martyred, and the Baron kidnaps Carla, who longs for Orgone. Turzahnelle and Orgone are ferried by Charon without either knowing of the other's presence, but a shipwreck deposits them on a cannibal island where the Baron is chief cook. Turzahnelle exclaims, 'My cook is goosed', as the cook gooses her. Seated on a toilet throne, she reviews a parade of flagellants climaxed by a radiant Vera: '*Choirs of angels sing joyously as the curtain falls.*' My summary is more linear than the actual performance, with its song, dance, parades, slapstick, quick changes of scene and costume, and improvisation so free that performance time varied between three and four hours.

Beginning with *Bluebeard*, however, the Ridiculous Theatrical Company inserted its typical pansexual *lazzi* (tricks) into a more coherent plot. A combination of Gothic novel, science fiction and heroic tragedy, *Bluebeard* offered its writer the title role. Bluebeard marries and destroys women, but he does so in the cause of science: 'If only there were some new and gentle genital that would combine with me, and mutually interpenetrated, steer me through this storm in paradise!' Among his con-genital failures is Lamia the Leopard-Woman (originally played by transvestite Mario Montez) and Maggot, his slave. The play opens as the good ship *Lady Vain* deposits Bluebeard's innocent victim, Sybil, who is accompanied by her fiancé Rodney Parker and her malapropism-spouting governess. Avid for guinea pigs, Bluebeard marries both the women. After successful surgery that grafts a chicken-

141

claw genital on Sybil, who proves to be the daughter of Maggot, the visitors depart. Bluebeard is left to the tender ministrations of Lamia and Sheemish, determined to raise him from mediocrity: 'Come', they parody the Wilbur translation of *The Misanthrope*, 'let us do the best we can to change the opinion of this unhappy man.' The cast has done its best to change *our* opinion, about 'normal' sex.

The Ridiculous Theatrical Company's main vehicle for fun has been burlesque – of the film *Grand Hotel* in *Big Hotel* (1967), of Marlowe's *Tamburlaine* in *When Queens Collide* (1968), of Christian epics in *Whores of Babylon* (1968) and *Turds of Hell* (1969), of H. G. Wells's novel in *Bluebeard* (1970), of the Hatfield–McCoy feud in *Corn* (1972), of television police serials in *Hot Ice* (1974), of Wagner's *Ring* in *Der Ring Gott Farblonjet* (1977), and of Molière's *Bourgeois gentilhomme* in *Le Bourgeois avant-garde* (1983). Ludlam's most popular piece has been *Camille* (1973), where the burlesque is unwontedly muted. Although subtitled 'A Travesty on *La Dame aux camélias*', one-liners are rare: 'There are only two ways a woman may rise from the gutter and become a queen: prostitution or the stage.' Although it is easy to imagine a camp performance of the sentimental drama of Dumas *fils*, Ludlam played it with restrained feeling, and Steven Samuels declares, 'At every one of the more than 500 performances he gave over seven years, he brought his audiences directly from laughter to tears.' Be that as it may, not until ten years later did Ludlam write another woman's role for himself (that of the opera diva in *Galas*).

Despite large chunks of undigested *Hamlet*, *Stage Blood* (1975) mutes burlesque and transsexuality. In Stefan Brecht's description it is 'a not altogether ridiculous because somewhat sincere *Hamlet*, dedicated to the insincerity of the actor and to the love homosexual sons bear their ridiculous fathers'. This seems to me to impose seriousness on a touring production of *Hamlet* as viewed from the (un)dressing-rooms. A local girl Ophelia is rehearsed by Ludlam/Hamlet, whose Stage Manager lover is also a playwright. When Ludlam's father, the Actor–Manager/Ghost, is murdered, his wife Gertrude wants her lover, the practical joker Claudius, to rule the company. After a series of reversals, the Ghost returns to life, claims Ophelia as his mistress, promotes his wife's lover, accepts his son's lover's play for production, and orders more stage blood.

By 1980 the core members of the Ridiculous Theatrical Company had played together through thick and mostly thin for some thirteen years. The group disbanded, but Ludlam continued his frenetic pace and in the next five years wrote a dozen plays, plus filmscripts and librettos, while continuing to act and direct. Having achieved financial security for the first time in his life, he learned in 1986 that he was ill with AIDS. Although he fought the disease with a macrobiotic diet and a relaxation of his work schedule, Charles Ludlam died in 1987 at the age of forty-four. His work continues to be played without him.

Much of gay theatre glints with light surfaces. Under them Duberman and Patrick plead for sexual acceptance. Under them Tavel and Ludlam burlesque sexist society and its reflection in the stereotypes of sexist art. At the end of the 1960s both these writers graduated from merry pansexual bedlams to more coherent characters moving through more linear plots. Those of Tavel strained toward philosophy, whereas those of Ludlam romped through farce. The Ridiculous was decreasingly outrageous. In contrast, Bernard's plays decimate plot and character to theatricalise moments of torture at the limit of the bearable. Bernard's metaphoric queers enter Artaud's Theatre of

Cruelty. With curious prescience, Albee's intermittently cruel Martha announced this grave gay theatre: 'I have a fine sense of the ridiculous but no sense of humor.'

Other gay theatre of the 1980s has entered the mainstream through two tributaries – entertainment and AIDS. Harvey Fierstein's one-acters are spliced into a trilogy around each of these themes – *Torch Song Trilogy* (1981) and *Safe Sex* (1987). Terence McNally's *Lisbon Traviata* (1989) belongs in the first group and Larry Kramer's *Normal Heart* in the second. More than the other arts, the theatre has alerted audiences to the contemporary AIDS plague, and every play with that purpose is commendable.

I began this chapter with an editor's definition of gay theatre. That editor, William Hoffman, was also a playwright, with over a dozen productions to his credit. Only a few of his plays have been published, however, and they reveal someone still in search of a style. Ironically, his AIDS play *As Is* (1985) has crowned his career. When the writer Rich learns he has AIDS, he is on the point of separation from his photographer lover Saul. As Rich falls increasingly prey to the plague, we witness a gamut of reactions topped by the unswerving devotion of Saul: 'I'll take you as is.' Hoffman interweaves the clinical symptoms of AIDS into the atmosphere of gay life in the fast lane. He shifts mercurially from waspish witticisms to an anonymous chorus; he moves back and forth in time. And who can blame him if he finally loses his nerve and ends on an optimistic note?

AIDS remains virulent at the beginning of the 1990s, and that ferocious fact casts its icy light on gay and ridiculous alike.

9
Visuals, and Visions:
Foreman, Breuer

This chapter hazards the most problematic aspect of contemporary divergent dramaturgy, which woos the eye as much as the ear. Certain Americans have forged influential visual modes in theatre: Peter Schuman of the Bread and Puppet Theatre; Robert Wilson, originally of the Byrd Hoffman Foundation; Richard Schechner of the Performance Group; Richard Foreman of the Ontological Hysteric Theatre; Lee Breuer and JoAnne Akalaitis of the Mabou Mines; and Liz Lecompte of the Wooster Group. All have published scripts, but the text is only one element of these contemporary avatars of Wagner's *Gesamtkunstwerk* – arts blended in performance. In traditional terminology they resemble directors rather than dramatists. The critic Bonnie Marranca grouped Breuer, Foreman and Wilson as Theatre of Images, but Foreman and Breuer speak of themselves as playwrights, and both have published collections of their texts, which are beginning to be performed outside their particular theatres, with other casts. Although Breuer and Foreman are steeped in the visual arts, their plays abound in words. I appreciate the inadequacy of commenting only on their words when the visual engulfs the verbal in performance, sometimes drowning it. We are, however, not in performance but in print.

Richard Foreman was born in New York City in 1937. While still in high school, he happened upon the works of Brecht, and was indelibly marked by that playwright's 'estrangement effect'. After graduating from Brown University, Foreman enrolled in John Gassner's playwriting programme at Yale University, and he still speaks fondly of that critic, against whose aesthetic he reacted. But slowly. While still at Yale, Foreman cast longing eyes toward Broadway, and, by his own account, his plays were tailored to suit. Upon receiving his degree, Foreman moved to New York City, where he entered the playwriting wing of the Actors Studio. In his own (rather jaundiced) words about this period, 'One year I imitated Arthur Miller, the next year Brecht, the next year Giraudoux.' Mildly interested in the Living Theatre, he was energised by the underground movies shown in that theatre's building. Foreman found the film-makers' dislocation of time and space a challenge to his perceptions and a reflection of his own thoughts. He decided to try to stage such dislocations with techniques analogous to those used by Jack Smith, Yvonne Rainer and, later, Andy Warhol. Filmmaker Jonas Mekas offered Foreman a site – the Cinematheque on Wooster Street in New York's SoHo. Foreman baptised his theatre even before it was born with the flashy direction-pointer 'Ontological/Hysteric', which he later described:

I have always dealt with basically nineteenth-century classic theatrical situations, like boulevard comedy triangles and so forth, and tried to redeem those [hysterical] situations by atomising them, by breaking them apart and letting other considerations bleed through. Those other considerations being, in essence, philosophical, ontological considerations.

Foreman has written some fifty plays, directing them himself but classifying only a fraction of them as Ontological/ Hysteric Theatre. Most of these were produced between 1975 and 1979 in his own loft, with the audience confined to seven rows of uncomfortable risers at one end of a long room. His plays of the 1980s have been produced in Paris and several places in New York.

Although Foreman's interviews, essays, and manifestos readily parade his theory, he insists, 'After the fact, I do much theorizing, and *alongside* the fact, I do much theorizing, but things [performances] never come from theorizing directly.' Desiring to deconstruct traditional (hysterical) drama, Foreman draws his material from a notebook in which he writes continuously. Like Gertrude Stein, whose plays he saw performed at the Judson Memorial Church in the early 1960s, he is obsessed by processes of consciousness, and, like her, that is what he seeks to render in his scripts.

Although he has functioned 'as composer, designer, writer, director, dance director, you know, everything', Foreman considers that his verbal text is at the centre of

a theatre which broke down all elements into a kind of atomic structure – and showed those elements of story, action, sound, light, composition, gesture, in terms of the smallest building-block units, the basic cells of the perceived experience of both living and art-making. The scripts themselves read like notations of my own process of imagining a theatre piece.

The scripts may read that way to their author, who is re-reading his own thoughts, but they are almost impenetrable to the reader who has not, and often even to someone who has, experienced them in the theatre. Although the story-line has often been slighted in Off-Off-Broadway productions, almost no one jettisons it as totally as Foreman (after Gertrude Stein). Upon his Stein base of random associations in the unconscious, a continuous present, Foreman builds 'decentred structures'. Brecht, Stein, underground films and post-structuralist criticism combine in Foreman's art to pulverise plot and emotional characters. Replacing Aristotelian plot and character with manipulation of space and space-fillers, Foreman is willy-nilly in Artaud's lineage as well as that of Brecht. More modestly, perhaps, he envisions changing civilisation through an audience who will absorb thought by perception:

> I want to refocus the attention of the spectator on the intervals, gaps, relations and rhythms which saturate the objects (acts and physical props) which are the 'givens' of any particular play. In doing this, I believe the spectator is made available (as I am, hopefully, when writing) to those most desirable energies which secretly connect him (through a kind of resonance) with the foundations of his being.

Foreman's plotless Ontological/Hysteric plays progress from moment to moment, by tableaux rather than incidents; as in film, his continuity consists of frames, and frequent transformations of the visual field recall the jump-cuts of film. His plays sometimes take sonata form: A–B–A, or frenzy – almost unbearable slow motion – frenzy. Movement is pervasive, sometimes slight (during the long B section), sometimes tumultuous (A and C), each testing the spectator's powers of perception. The reader, as distinguished from the spectator, must imagine manipulation of space and time: *space* in framing devices through scenic directions about doors, windows, mirrors, or moving planes, and strings that impose attachments while outlining configurations; *time* in scenic directions about thuds, buzzers, metronomes, raucous music, bare or strobe lights, and, masquerading as dialogue, wordless exclamations or meaningless repetitions. Moreover, the printed plays do not indicate when a character speaks 'live' or in voice-over. On the other hand, the texts *are* in print, and the reader or director is free to betray Foreman's own models of production.

In performance Foreman visibly controls lights, sounds and incessant changes of set. Although he does not manipulate his actors on stage (like the Polish sculptor–director Tadeusz Kantor), he treats his actors like found objects. Conversely, objects may acquire quasi-human personality – lamps in *Total Recall*, rocks in *Hotel China*, doll-houses in *Sophia III*. 'People are more interesting than props', a voice-over announces in *Sophia*, but Foreman's plays question the assertion. Scenic intricacies replace story intricacies, and through them runs a dialogue which is only sporadically communicative, composed of flat dry works that the characters mouth in flat dry tones. However, though Foreman jettisons dramatic plot, he thrives on the battle of the sexes, in which woman lures man from his creative destiny.

The corpus of Foreman's Ontological/Hysteric Theatre is full of repetition: *Sophia* = *Wisdom* is the title of four plays; other titles repeat puns – *Pain(t)*, *MISrepresentation*, *Fall-starts*. From play to play the same characters reappear – clumsy Max the writer, his *alter ego* Ben the lover, another *alter ego* Leo, his seductive girlfriend Rhoda, her jealous rivals Hannah and Eleanor, her friends and helpers Ida and Sophia – and the women often appear nude. The repetition of framing and punctuating devices is at once familiar and inventive; playing with planes is the stable, unstable ground of Foreman's drama. Although he abjures plots and inveighs against interpretation, his polarities are insistent – man versus woman, garments versus nakedness, mind versus body, writing versus being, words versus things. To keep his 'action at a distance' – a play title – Foreman glances parodically at painting, literature, film, philosophy, and he makes 'in' jokes at his own expense: 'Text, text, that's what counts. Not music, not ideas, not decor'; 'Oh, my happiness is complete when I can relate the thing that I am seeing to the thing that I am hearing'; 'Subtlety is not perhaps my forte.'

Foreman closed his loft in 1979, but the Ontological/ Hysteric Theatre moves with him. It is pointless to apply traditional critical shorthand to this work, skimming a number of plays to linger on one that is typical or celebrated or fine. I could say, for example, that *Angelface* (1968) introduces Foreman's characters and devices, with Rhoda (played always by Kate Manheim) appearing in wings; that *Total Recall* (1970) is the boast of Ben, who plays mind to Leo's body while Sophia hides under Hannah's nightgown; that *Hotel China* (1971) is at once sexuality and language, cold and fragile under the impact of theatre rocks. *Sophia = Wisdom: Part 3, the Cliffs* (1971) probably exhibits Foreman's greatest control of his theatre idiom: Rhoda and Ben are the naked views of Sophia and Max, with Hannah and Karl performing in trivial everyday relationships; through the inventive manipulation of cliff-boxes and sexually suggestive props, the male–female rivalries emerge sharply in spite of flat acting. Stefan

Brecht has extensively analysed *Particle Theory* (1972) as a reply to *Cliffs*. Foreman himself reads *Pandering to the Masses* (1974) as

> the relation between knowing and dying to habit and convention; *Rhoda in Potatoland* [1974] on the physicality and urge to tumescence of all 'body-things' as they try to swamp mind-things in us; *Book of Splendors* [1977] on the world experienced as pure 'multiplicity' and the mind's effort to steer clearly through, and using, that multiplicity.

Foreman forges ahead with his own distinctive idiom in his plays of the 1980s – strings, ropes, objects, buzzers and lights framing and punctuating the flat lines of dialogue. In print, however, the plays sport few of the typographical signs that make one conscious of the reading-process. *Book of Splendors* already introduced the actual names of the actors, but *Penguin Touquet* (1981) prints those names rather than the invented Rhoda–Max–Ben, the hysterical triangle. *Café Amérique* (1981) and *Egyptology* (1983) no longer assign specific lines to specific characters, although the actors in production clearly 'owned' their lines. *The Cure* (1986) implies a cathartic promise: 'The pain is the cure.' Foreman's final play of the 1980s, *Lava* (1989, not yet published as I write), is unusually explicit in rendering language visible: augmenting his obsessive phrasal repetition by live actors and voice-over, one woman writes phrases on two different blackboards throughout the play, the male actors are lost in large books, and an oscilloscope front and centre shows us the shape of the speeches we hear. Rather than molten rock, our theatre world erupts in a lava of molten words.

For over two decades Richard Foreman has explored

the theatre to subvert theatre. Framing his plays to mock Renaissance perspective, subjecting his characters to nine-teenth-century triangular hysteria, flattening his dialogue to simple phrases, he pursues a vision not only of decon-struction but of detheatricalisation of theatre, while high-lighting the visuality of the ordinary properties and extraordinary technology of the modern theatre.

Perhaps it would be illuminating to conclude on Fore-man's contrast between theatre of the past and his own:

Old paradigm: Universe consists of forces that solidify into units (Gestalts, objects, events) to which we *respond*.

New paradigm: Universe consists of forces that leave traces which are not fully identifiable consciously, of which we see only residual evidence – and if we respond it is 'error' of responding to what we *project* into those traces.

If you believe 1, your art tries to make something visible, and the life copied by that art is a responding-to-input from the 'world'.

If you believe 2, your (my) art tries to erase things (because they are obstacles) and the life copied by that art is a 'something else' that tries to resonate to inner output.

The work of the Mabou Mines Company, and particu-larly of Lee Breuer, might fall between the two paradigms. This company's art is certainly a 'something else' taking a myriad of forms 'to resonate to inner input', and their art also deals in unsettling perceptions spatially and tem-porally, but they deliberately leave the traces, encouraging a projection from the spectators, eliciting an emotional response. Influenced, like Foreman, by Brecht's distancing of the performance, the Mabou Mines do not reject the Stanislavski-based Method of emotional memory. Attuned like Foreman to art movements such as Minimalism and Conceptualism, the Mabou Mines never treat actors as objects, but at once as expressive instruments and virtuosos who play on those instruments.

Their principal playwright is Lee Breuer, born, like Foreman, in 1937, but coming to maturity 3000 miles away in Los Angeles, with an awareness of Hollywood *kitsch*. A university graduate, like Foreman, Breuer studied English literature because he thought that a would-be playwright should read omnivorously, but he spent most of his time in the theatre, where he met actress Ruth Maleczech, whom he later married. (Foreman lives with his main actress, Kate Manheim.) University-trained, immersed in literature, Breuer and Foreman wrote their first plays for more or less commercial outlets – Breuer winning a national award and Foreman having a play optioned for production on Broadway. As Brecht, then Stein, magnetised Foreman, Beckett attracted Breuer, who hitch-hiked from Los Angeles to San Francisco in order to see the Actor's Workshop production of *Waiting for Godot* in 1956. Disappointed at its bareness, he nurtured an opposition attitude toward the drama of the Absurd, wishing to see plays produced in arresting colours, lights, shapes, textures, harmonies; even before Foreman, he was yearning for a *Gesamtkunstwerk*. As Foreman savoured the experiments of underground film-makers, Breuer was on the fringes of the experimental San Francisco Tape Music Center of Morton Subotnik and Pauline Oliveros. He also worked with Ronnie Davis soon after the founding of the San Francisco Mime Troupe, for whom he directed parts of the *Caucasian Chalk Circle*, to which he invited composers, dancers, visual artists. In that milieu Breuer met actors JoAnne Akalaitis and Bill Raymond, who later helped create the Mabou Mines.

With their taste for the modern European classics, the Breuers left in 1965 for Europe, where, to their surprise, they remained five years, meeting the other members of what was to become the Mabou Mines Company. Living on odd jobs, they pursued theatre activities, but Breuer's role shifted from playwright to director – of Brecht and Beckett. Only when they returned to the States did they found the Mabou Mines Company, named after the Nova Scotia town where JoAnne Akalaitis offered them rehearsal space, and where they began to create collective pieces, with Breuer supplying the words: 'I've been using theatre to hide that I'm really a writer.'

Breuer views his *Animations* as steps toward a cycle of six Realms which dramatise 'a story of an unenlightened life'. The titles – *The Red Horse Animation* (1970, revised 1972), *The B. Beaver Animation* (1974) and *The Shaggy Dog Animation* (1978) – reveal his reliance on the beast-fable tradition, which is at least as old as Aesop. The titles also suggest modern film technology: an animation conveys an impression of motion through rapid scanning of stills. And of course 'animation' means vivacity. As published, the *Animations* do not reveal which actor speaks which line of dialogue, and there are no scenic directions. The text itself appears in block capital letters, punctuated only by stops.

Originally played by three actors, *The Red Horse Animation* opens in three printed columns that Breuer calls tracks: Outline, Lifeline, Storyline. Some third of the way through the piece, however, Lifeline and Storyline merge. The three columns begin with avatars of the same question: 'Why pretend?' or 'Why make art?' The script is its own nebulous answer, whose movement is a rising action, a culmination and a rather swift fall. The Outline, as is fitting, worries about form and shape; the Lifeline veers from the physical lifeline in the palm of a hand to the metaphysical line of spiritlife; the Storyline blends an American boyhood with a romantic dream of red horses crossing the Gobi Desert in the time of Genghis Khan. Each red horse bears a message wrapped around an arrow; he is driven to the limit of endurance before the message is transferred to another horse. When Lifeline and Storyline join, to the punctuation of cinematic cuts and pans, the horse wonders about the message, and the text closes in on one such horse, quoting Beckett: 'HOW I HOLD ME IN MY ARMS AND TELL ME A STORY.'

Much of the story is about the red horse's sire, Daily Bread, a pun on money and the staff of life, fitted with blinkers, tied to a pole, and compelled to circle endlessly on the thresher floor – 'A HORSE'S ASS'. The Outline returns to the red horse, whose Life and Storylines are a continuous *line*, in reaction against the circles of Daily Bread, the humdrum sire. With illness, the red horse sees himself as mere representation; the figure of a red horse can no longer contain him. Condensed, witty, punning visually and verbally, the play plunges an equine metaphor into the surround of modern electronic and cinematic technology, to create the portrait of the artist as a young theatre.

B. Beaver is a very different animal, accompanied in performance by his family, but the actors are also objects and natural forces. Busy as his proverbial ancestor, B. Beaver tells his own story in the wider of two printed columns. The other erupts in occasional sardonic commentary or scenic directions. Breuer labels them TEXT and TAKES – again the cinematic vocabulary. The red horse reacts against the life style of his sire, but B. Beaver rages against the elements that threaten his dam (a three-way pun).

He writes for do-it-yourself help on his dam: 'I AM A BEAVER WHO HAS LOST THE ART OF DAMNATION AT A CRUCIAL TIME.' But there is no reply. Confused but reasoning like Beckett's Unnamable, he puns in sorrow at the rush of spring: 'GET ON TOP OF WHAT'S UP. GET RIGHT TO THE BOTTOM OF WHAT'S GOING DOWN.' He battles with a trout in an extended prize-fight conceit. He wins, with assistance from the *Book of Job* – an example of 'A SPECIES IN EXTREMITIES'.

To protect his dam, B. Beaver stutters through an arsenal of modern slang and puns; the vocabularies of geology, zoology, boxing; a few dashes of Latin and a few more of Beckett, But the dam bursts, and a last sardonic comment informs us that B. Beaver ends up as a Wino on Second Avenue. As the red horse sought form, B. Beaver wanted to strengthen his dam, but the verbal force explodes the set (literally) to dramatise the vanity of the melting snows of spring, the vanity of an artist dam(n)ed in his medium.

Most ambitious of Breuer's animations is *The Shaggy Dog*, about four times as long as either of the others, some four hours in the Mabou mines performance, involving eight actors and a puppet. The text as published bifurcates into Sound and Image Tracks, and it too uses a beast fable (even though a shaggy dog is a fictitious beast) to dramatise the life of the artist, in three parts. On the page the Sound Track, a broad column in Breuer's customary capital letters, takes epistolary form, for a correspondence addressed to movie cameraman John Greed by Rose / shaggy dog / puppet / movie-cutter. Having left John, Rose writes him a letter that flashes back to their meeting, to her puppy love for him, and to her rivalry with 'that female person' Leslie. The Image Track, in contrast, is never epistolary, but descriptive, sardonic, meditative in self-address by

Rose. It reduces the love scene to camera specifics, and Part I ends in a rush of contemporary sitcom clichés about lovers parting.

In Part II the odd couple have separated, and we follow Rose. While the Image Track hides Rose's misery in recipes, the Sound Track delivers a history of dogs as domesticated animals. The Sound Track then recounts Rose's affair with Bunny, but on the Image Track she talks movie language with Ed. Back in New York City she surprises herself with a litter by the dog Broadway. Having to make a living, Rose enters the art world: 'I LEARNED TO SHAKE HANDS. PLAY DEAD. AND BEG. TWO WEEKS LATER I PICKED UP A CAPS GRANT. . . . SPEAKING PUBLICLY I PICKED UP A BARK WORSE THAN MY BITE.' In a hilarious parody of critical jargon, Rose retires from the art market. She tries to recapture her life with John, but near a garbage truck they again take leave of one another, to end Part II.

In Part III Rose reads about John's offer of a reward for a lost dog, with a three-year-old picture of her. She has her own life on the Sound Track; on the Image Track, John as puppet at first speaks to two different people on two different phones, but soon he narrows down to himself as professional movie-maker talking shop and through it revealing his artistic desperation. Ending without ending the telephone conversation, the play reverts to the Sound Track – first a recitation of clichés about trying to renounce an obsessive habit, and then a retreat into the unconscious for the dog/artist/lover who should know better but doesn't. Finally, rhymingly, Rose declares her independence: 'WRONG LIFE BABY. NEXT TIME. MAYBE. I TELL YOU THE TRUTH. ONLY SLEEPING DOGS LIE.' And sleeping is not for hyperactive shaggy dog Rose, who has plunged us in truths through her tricks and tracks.

Rose the shaggy dog (originally played by a Bunraku-type puppet designed by Linda Hartinian) dominates her *Animation*, but her master, John Greed, also played by a large puppet, was salvaged by Breuer for *Prelude to Death in Venice* (1980). The Thomas Mann story is quoted in Breuer's play, but death in Venice is also the failure to shoot a movie in Venice, California. Visually, we see an actor (Bill Raymond) dressed like the puppet John and manoeuvring him back and forth between two telephone booths. 'Hang on a sec' is the leitmotiv of the puppet-master Bill, the puppet John, and his film agent Bill Morris. *Prelude* resembles the *Animations* in its blend of esoteric references and double-edged slang, but it seems more acutely tuned to popular culture.

1983 witnessed the production of two searching Breuer works – the monologue *Hajj* and the first version of *The Gospel at Colonus*. The printed text of *Hajj* (meaning a pilgrimage to Mecca) divides between complex scenic directions and the words to be spoken. An actress applies make-up with her back to the audience. Closed-circuit television monitors her associations, and tapes superimpose images from her past. The performer becomes actress, daughter, mother, whore, child, dervish, old man. We gradually piece together the story of a father who shot himself before his daughter could pay the sum she owed him – a literal and symbolic debt. But the daughter is an actress; father and son live in her performance of extraordinary visual complexity.

One of the most original voices on the modern American stage, Breuer paradoxically received a playwriting award for *The Gospel at Colonus*, most of the words in which were penned by Robert Fitzgerald, poet and translator of Sophocles. In Breuer's only popular success (a success even on Broadway) blind Oedipus is transplanted to a Pentecostal Gospel church; Bob Telson wrote music appropriate to the setting and Breuer supplied the lyrics. The old classic became magnificently colourful in this impassioned rendition.

As a playwright, Breuer is unique in his blend of erudite reference, jive talk and technological innovation. The obverse of Foreman in his dedication to fable, however fragmented, Breuer resembles him in rendering visual a new vision of art, which never claims modernist privilege for that art. Breuer weaves a story through his intricate actions, and Foreman imprisons his characters in myriad scenic activities. Although their printed texts reveal much less than traditional playscripts about the perceptual complexities of performance, they still send the imagination soaring, and Breuer is funny to boot.

10
Eloquent Energies: Mamet, Shepard

There is no dearth of doom-sayers for American drama. In the 1960s action-performance (analogous to action-painting) displaced dramaturgy in the avant-garde. In the 1970s a Theatre of Images gleamed more brightly than theatre of words. In the 1980s, however, two major American playwrights created major dramas, so doom must be delayed.

In a time of newly emergent voices (which I have tried to present) I remain appreciative of the sheer quality of the most telling plays of David Mamet and Sam Shepard. Male playwrights who dramatise masculine competitive worlds, they are similar in activating characters who sizzle in performance. Aristotle would bemoan their disjunctive plots, rich in the middle but thin at beginning and end. Less explicitly than their common ancestor Eugene O'Neill, they depict a materialistic United States that has strayed from or deliberately corrupted its potential. The theme is common to almost every serious American writer, but Mamet and Shepard infuse their dark visions with a comic distillate. Their little people live in a large country, and their bristling dialogues expand the stage. Born four years apart into unstable family situations – 'I come from a Broken Home. The most important institution in America', as Mamet put it – they have developed distinctive voices. Mamet is an urban, vituperative miniaturist, whereas Shepard is a ranging, musical myth-maker.

Born in a Chicago suburb in 1947, Mamet was involved in theatre as early as high school. Although he held odd jobs through college, he worked at Second City backstage, and he later appropriated the revue format of two counterpointed characters in short, swiftly paced scenes.

While still at college, Mamet began to compose skits and plays, and he studied acting at the Neighborhood Playhouse, where he learned to 'play the moment'. As an instructor, he wrote *Lakeboat* (1970 but later revised), which he had claimed as an opus before it was written, and for an amateur acting company he wrote *Duck Variations* (1971), which was later professionally produced in Chicago.

In *Duck Variations*, as in Albee's *Zoo Story* a decade earlier, two men meet on a park bench. As in the Theatre of the Absurd, Mamet's '*two gentlemen in their sixties*' are totally concentrated in their stage presence; their names are Emil Varec and George S. Aronovitz, but these are never used in the dialogue. They savour their surroundings on a fine spring day, particularly the ducks in the lake. George is dominatingly lyrical: he opens one 'variation' with the poignant but pithy generalisation, 'You know, the duck's life is not all hearts and flowers.' Subsequent 'variations' circle around the specifics of ducks' lives – their troubles, loneliness, migrations, societies, the dangers they face, exotic breeds. Emil dominates the final 'variation', conjuring centuries of bird-watchers, from the ancient

Greeks on: 'A fitting end. / To some very noble creatures of the sky. / And a lotta Greeks.' At once funny and sad, *Duck Variations* includes its own epitaph: 'A crumbling civilization and they're out in the Park looking at birds.' In the theatre, however, they're out on stage *talking* about birds – in a brilliantly stylised idiom.

Sexual Perversity in Chicago opened in Chicago in 1974, but soon moved to New York and London. The single act comprises thirty-four variations on the theme of sex. The four characters – two young men and two young women – are obsessed with sex, an obsession they express in careless obscenities and formulaic intimacies. In the first scene, set in a singles bar, two young males talk about sex; the elder of the two, Bernard Litko, describes a fantastic encounter to his friend Danny Shapiro. Some nine weeks later, on a beach, the same two friends ogle female bodies. During the summer Dan and Deb have fallen in love, lived together and separated. Their brief union has been marred by the callousness of Bernie toward Deb, by the hostility to Dan of Deb's friend Joan. When Deb returns to the flat she shared with Joan, she admits her own fault. On the beach, neither young stud mentions Deb. When an attractive (but invisible) woman does not respond to their greeting, Danny explodes, 'Deaf *Bitch*', venting his frustration at what he has lost.

The 'sexual perversity' of the title is a refusal to invest sexual relations with affection. Structured in swift scenes that rise like dirty jokes to punch-lines, the play is almost barren of setting, although it moves through bars, offices, dwellings and a beach. These nominal locales are sounding-boards for sexuality. The cult of the cool governs human relations. As the conversation of *Duck Variations* reveals and assuages the fundamental loneliness of two old men, so the conversation of *Sexual Perversity* reveals but does not assuage the fundamental emptiness of four young people. And to each Mamet supplies an accurate idiom.

The idiom changes in *American Buffalo*, which arrived on Broadway in 1977. Conversation is again front and centre, although the characters are petty hoodlums. Mamet achieves freshness even in tough talk: 'Only, and I'm not, I don't think, casting anything on anyone: from the mouth of a Southern bulldyke asshole ingrate of a vicious nowhere cunt can this trash come.' The American buffalo is the buffalo-headed nickel found in Don's junk-shop, which inspires a fantasy crime against its purchaser – a crime masterminded by Don for performance by Bob. Teach appears in Don's shop and persuades him to let him replace Bob in the action, and by extension in Don's friendship. Near midnight, as the time for the robbery approaches, Bob appears with another buffalo nickel. His presence embarrasses Don and irritates Teach, who hits the young man. Bob confesses that *he* bought the valuable nickel, invented the rich coin-collector and suggested the burglary. In frustration, Teach smashes up Don's shop and then, subdued, prepares to take Bob to the hospital for his injured ear – the ear that Teach injured. Don then apologises to Bob, and Bob to Don, who assures him that he 'did real good'. American buffalo is human as well as nickel in the tough talk that 'buffaloes' the meek, who inherit nothing.

Like *American Buffalo, A Life in the Theatre* (1977) opened at Chicago's Goodman Theater and then moved on to New York. This play too circles round to its beginning. In both the first and last scenes an older actor and a younger actor wish each other 'Goodnight' and then leave the theatre. In the first scene, however, young John is deferential to experienced Robert; by the last scene, John is better known and borrows money from Robert, who, alone, murmurs, 'The lights dim. Each to his own home.' But their true home is the theatre, which Mamet dramatises in skilful vignettes of hackneyed Broadway or Hollywood acting vehicles – in the trenches, in Elizabethan garb, caught in adultery, in death throes, in a lifeboat, in the surgery; through these scenes thread missed cues, forgotten lines, broken props, against the steady rise of a younger actor and fall of an older one. Mamet's infallible ear captures the careless artifice and the offstage rhetoric of professionals in a life as superficial as their calling, and yet Mamet fails to intimate that superficiality rather than nostalgia for the trite old scenes.

As *A Life in the Theatre* revives old theatre scenes, *The Water Engine* (1977) revives old radio, the medium for which it was originally written. A 1930s radio play is set in a 1970s studio; the inventor of an engine that will run on water is assassinated by vested interests threatened by the invention. Interrupting this play of another era are announcements about chain letters, snatches of 1930s music, barkers for the 1934 Chicago World's Fair. The frame play gently mocks a World's Fair predicting a century of progress, while the inventor of an ecological miracle is annihilated.

Reunion (1977) turns back from the social to the personal; it ends, as the title implies, in person-to-person warmth. A fifty-three-year-old father has a reunion with his twenty-five-year-old daughter, whom he abandoned years ago. In contrast to *Duck Variations*, lacking all exposition, *Reunion* consists almost wholly of delayed exposition. Father has had several jobs, several women, too much alcohol. Daughter is married to and working for an older man with two children. Finally, father presents daughter with a bracelet, and they go to dinner together, loneliness assuaged – for the time being.

The Woods (1977) is almost Dantean – in the middle of a life, self-discovery in a dark wood. Mamet dramatises the middle of a love affair, with self-discovery in a run-down summer house near the woods. Nick and Ruth, city lovers, go there to be alone. The house belongs to Nick, and urbanite Ruth is determined to relish the country flora, fauna and atmosphere. She relishes loquaciously, recalling her grandmother, whose bracelet she has lost. Nervous Nick thinks of his father, who spent a night during the Second World War in a fox hole with a madman who later visited the family in this very house. Though each member of the couple repeats 'Tell me', they are self-absorbed.

During a storm, they drink, quarrel, revert to recollections of father and grandmother. Their rapport is at a low point when Ruth gives Nick a bracelet inscribed with her eternal love. In the morning their nerves are raw, and Ruth has packed to leave. Their quarrel explodes into violence, with Nick on the verge of madness. Yet they finally cling together, and Ruth again tries to comfort Nick with her grandmother's story of two children lost in the woods. Both in and outside the story, it is not at all certain that comfort is attained, for Mamet subdues our laughter at his couple in order to delineate a loneliness that can be assuaged only momentarily – if at all.

In the 1980s Mamet emerged as a major playwright, in spite of his limited palette. Of his plays of the period *Edmond* (1982) is probably the most searching and (there-fore?) the least successful commercially. The sexist, racist, homophobic protagonist leaves his middle-class marriage in quest of a different life. Meeting with greed, sexual frustration, murderous violence, he is jailed. In prison he is sodomised by his black cell-mate, but when he reports this to the chaplain he is simply urged to repent. In the final scene Edmond achieves harmony as the willing, vulnerable companion of his nameless cell-mate.

In a brilliant analysis, Dennis Carroll has linked Mamet's rhythmic language in *Edmond* to the three-stage journey of Joseph Campbell's 'Hero with a Thousand Faces' – formal but hackneyed discourse during departure, abrupt obscenities during the initiation of his imagined release, and pause-marked inarticulacy followed by fluidity in his return to society. Although a two-prisoner cell is a very different society from Edmond's middle-class home – and therefore not quite a return – the play's linguistic variety shows Mamet in control of his medium.

That control is displayed more ostentatiously in *Glengarry Glen Ross* (1983), which also features Mamet's largest cast of characters – seven. The title refers not to the Scottish highlands but to Florida swamps, which high-pressure real-estate salesmen attempt to foist on gullible customers. The invisible owners of the enterprise spur competition among the salesmen: top prize is a Cadillac, second a set of steak knives, and the others will be fired.

Mamet dextrously interweaves a plot mystery with revelation of character. Rhythmic shifts are indicative not of a hero's quest, but of degrees of insecurity. Williamson is a petty office tyrant with no experience as a salesman, and he is literally tight-lipped, lacing his phrases with casual obscenities. Roma is the shrewd and personable champion, who sells his friendship along with property – equally worthless – but his verbal arias are bejewelled with imaginative obscenities. Moss, Aaronow and Levene are older, wearier and more desperate. They speak similarly in an argot of questions, elisions, interruptions and pleonastic obscenities. Moss conceives an office robbery for the crucial 'leads' (to customers). He enlists Aaronow's aid, but the robbery is actually performed – and inadvertently revealed (to Williamson and us) – by the hapless Levene.

In a final irony, an ignorant Roma urges Levene to team up with him – just before he is apprehended by the police. But the partnership offer is spurious: 'My stuff is mine, his stuff is ours.'

More graphically than *American Buffalo*, *Glengarry Glen Ross* indicts the cut-throat competition of free enterprise, and yet the vigorous lexicon undercuts the moral stance. As Teach's picturesque prejudices mitigate his viciousness in *American Buffalo*, those of Roma become almost endearing. Moreover, our sympathy grows for Levene the Machine as he boasts of bilking an old couple, as he connives with Roma to defraud his client, as he tries to bribe Williamson. By the time Williamson explains his incrimination – 'Because I don't like you' – we *do* like Levene, for his brazen stupid bravery against all odds. In spite of the contradiction between energy and morality, *Glengarry Glen Ross* is Mamet's most skilful blend of theme, character, and idiom, which readily lends itself to symbolic condemnation of American capitalism.

It is almost as though Mamet alternates musical keys in his theatre work of the 1980s. The linear but relatively subdued quest of *Edmond* was followed by the verbal explosions of *Glengarry*, which was followed in turn by the softer melody of *The Shawl* (1985), after which *Speed-the-Plow* (1987) erupted. In *The Shawl* we do not see the title garment, but a medium John, having noted it on photographs of his client's mother, uses it to convince that client that he has made contact with her dead mother. The shawl becomes a metaphor for art: although John explains his profession to Charles, the final presence transcends his tricks: 'I do not know. That is all I saw.' It is enough to ensure his client's trust.

Trust, lack thereof, is at the centre of *Speed-the-Plow*. The barely localised or unlocalised settings of most Mamet plays here give way to Hollywood. As Frank Rich remarked in his review, 'Hell hath no fury like a screen-writer scorned . . . [leading to] the same scorched-earth policy toward Hollywood that Nathanael West first apotheosized in *The Day of the Locust*.' Mamet's locusts are blood brothers to the petty crooks of *American Buffalo* and hungry real-estate salesmen of *Glengarry* – blood brothers slavering for messes and messes of pottage.

Bobbie Gould has just been promoted to Head of Production. Charlie Fox, a studio underling he has known for many years, brings him a 'buddy prison' script that interests the current macho star. Together they exult at the fame and fortune guaranteed by the presence of the star, and they do so in the concentrated profanities that are at once their gestures of love and Mamet's signature: 'We're gonna kick the ass of a lot of them fucken' people.'

At first almost digressive, a courtesy read has been ordered for a novel about radiation by 'an Eastern Sissy Writer'. And almost digressive is their $500 bet that Bobbie can seduce Karen, the temporary secretary (originally played by Madonna). When Karen preaches principle to Bobbie, the self-styled 'Big Fat Whore', he gives her the book to read and asks her to deliver a report at his home that evening: 'and tell [Charlie] he owes me five hundred bucks'.

But the debt proves greater and lesser. In Act II Karen converts Bobbie to her principles, and Mamet converts no one to his tone. Impossible to take seriously, Karen's sermon, stiffened with actual quotation from the novel, is not only unfunny but tedious. In Act III Bobbie informs an incredulous Charlie that he is replacing the 'buddy prison' film with an adaptation of the novel on radiation. Charlie reacts mercurially with Mamet's most pungent vituperations, and he assaults Bobbie physically.

Shrewdly, Charlie damns Karen: 'You're nothing to her but what you can *do* for her.' As a last concession Charlie asks Karen, 'You came to his house with the preconception, you wanted him to greenlight the book. . . . If he had said "No", would you have gone to bed with him?' When she answers in the negative, Charlie quickly reclaims Bobbie. The two men are finally together in their own 'buddy prison' film. And Mamet has us revelling in their lascivious idiom.

In *Angel City*, Sam Shepard, too, shoots barbs at Hollywood and he too immerses all characters in its slime. But the exploited artist is a recurrent protagonist in Shepard's drama, whereas Mamet's hustlers share his own love of words. Mamet is an accomplished sharpshooter, and the metaphor suits his language. Shepard is an accomplished musician, and the metaphor fits his colloquial lyricism.

Produced Off-Off-Broadway at the age of nineteen, published and winner of an Obie at twenty-three, contracted to write a movie at twenty-five, subsidised at Lincoln Center at twenty-seven, contracted to act in a movie – for a six-figure sum – at thirty-five, admired by academics as well as rock fans, Sam Shepard would seem to be fortune's child. With over forty plays written, he has moved from early images of fragmentation to sustained theatre metaphors of a moribund civilisation. His recent plays are cast in the tragic shadow of Eugene O'Neill, and he resembles O'Neill too, in gravitating from experimental to more realistic forms.

Born on a Mid-Western army base in 1943, growing up mainly on a California ranch, arriving in New York City in the 1960s, living for three years in London, he has various landscapes at his disposal. Bored at school, a gifted percussionist, devoted to sports, Shepard naturally thinks in terms of popular rather than pedantic myths. In the loose Bohemianism of Greenwich Village in the 1960s, he tried song lyrics, brief vignettes and short plays. Three Obies in swift succession fixed his genre. (He now has Obies for eleven plays.) These early plays may change locale – indoors, outdoors, home or hotel – but the time is always now. In form, associative monologues are glued on to disjunctive exchanges; collage is an apt description.

Cowboys and *Rock Garden* (1964) were produced on a double bill at Off-Off-Broadway Theatre Genesis, and they carry themes and images that recur in Shepard's work, which is often dedicated to Western legend. He admires figures who 'didn't have any real rules' – not only cowboys, but rock stars, sports champions, drug visionaries, young men rebelling against family constraint.

Cowboys #2, a rewriting of his first play, does not dramatise the young outlaws he praises, but two young men in an unlocalised setting, who nourish their imaginations on cowboys. Throughout the brief play they alternate between their reality as young men in a contemporary city and roles as old cowboys from scenes of film Westerns. In their inevitable battle with Indians, the audience sees a construction saw-horse and hears the offstage sound of galloping horses – an audio-visual pun. Only as cowboy comrades do the two men achieve communion. In contrast, their contemporary reality imposes isolation, and each young man delivers a manic monologue – a device that will become Shepard's trademark. At the play's end they enact old cowboys threatened by blazing sun and vultures; they are joined on stage (but not in communication) by two young men in business suits, with scripts from which they monotonously read the opening lines of the play. Whereas the original two men are nourished by the popular cowboy myth, their contemporaries are locked into dull practicalities.

Shepard's first extant play brought him a first taste of success when it was bought by Kenneth Tynan for *Oh! Calcutta*. *Rock Garden* (1964) dramatises mutual incomprehension within a family – a theme that recurs over a decade later in Shepard's realistic trilogy. In *Rock Garden* an adolescent boy threads through three scenes in three rooms of a house. Scene 1 is silent as the boy and his sister sip milk, unnoticed by their father reading a magazine. In scene 2 the boy in underwear in a rocking-chair asks laconic, sometimes insidious questions of a garrulous woman in her bed. Three times she likens one of the boy's features to his father's or grandfather's, and each time he returns from an errand with clothing over the inherited feature. At the end of the scene the man in underwear replaces the boy, and the woman is reduced to monosyllables. In scene 3 father and son are both in underwear in their living-room. Like the woman in the second scene the man speaks a virtual monologue, punctuated only by the boy's laconic, insidious questions and occasional falls from his chair. The father airs a fantasy about a rock garden, and after a long pause the son spews forth a monologue about sexual pleasure, which knocks the man off his couch. A contemporary *Spring's Awakening*, the play ends on a verbal climax about sexual climax. Finally, stripped to underwear, father and son engage in a dialogue of the deaf. Man, woman, and boy sing the same refrains: 'I don't know. . . . You know?' without knowing one another.

This example of generation gap is unusual in Shepard's early collages, which revolve about people his own age. In his first two years as a playwright Shepard dramatises his contemporaries in telling caricatures of American reality. On simple but striking stage sets, young men and women act compulsively, without making conventional sense. Shepard's young people flex their lexical muscles in long arias. Inventive, associative, syntactically simple but image-laden, the monologues are often paced by a refrain, and they resemble traditional soliloquies in exploring the speaker's inner life.

A second group of plays begins with *La Turista* (1967), although Shepard also wrote a few further collages. In the main group, which may be labelled 'fantasy', mythic characters figure in sustained plots, surcharged with incident. In *La Turista* pop and ritual elements are blended and force-fed into a classic structure of plague and catharsis. A more probable blend is that of pop music and crime in *Melodrama Play* (1967). *Forensic and the Navigators* (1967) can barely contain its mixture of science fiction, political revolution, and satirised bureaucracy.

Although *La Turista* (written in Mexico under the influence of amphetamines and dysentery) is one of Shepard's first plays to sustain a plot, that plot is not linear since the second act obliquely mirrors the first. Shepard's title puns on the Spanish word for 'tourist' and the diarrhoea that afflicts tourists in Mexico. In a brightly coloured Mexican hotel room an American couple, Kent and Salem, suffer from this illness and severe sunburn. A native shoeshine boy also irritates them, and when Kent faints, Salem telephones for a doctor. Enter a witch-doctor and son who engage in an arcane ceremony that lasts throughout the act. The shoeshine boy translates their ritual for the *turistas*, dons Kent's cowboy costume, and is auctioned off before being wooed by Salem to return to the States with her. At the end of Act I Kent lies inert before the chanting witch-doctor and his son. Act II finds Kent and Salem again in a hotel room, but this one sports American plastic. Kent is ill with sleeping sickness, behaving as if in a trance. This time Salem's SOS brings a father–son team behaving like country doctors of Western films, replete with drawl. On Doc's order, Salem and his son (played by the shoeshine boy of Act 1) keep Kent walking, but the drama gradually narrows down to a verbal duel between Doc and Kent.

In a face-off where Doc uses a real gun and Kent an imaginary one, the two men circle one another, Kent verbally transforming into a hunted monster. Suiting action to description, Kent leaps off the stage and runs behind the audience, where he assumes a dual role of prey and hunter. Moreover, the two antagonists exchange roles. After a series of verbal barrages, the play's end is strikingly gestural; Kent eludes Salem and Sonny by swinging Tarzan-like over the heads of the audience and on to the stage. He then '*runs straight toward the upstage wall of the set and leaps right through it, leaving a cut-out silhouette of his body in the wall*'.

The names of Kent and Salem, well-known brands of American cigarettes, suggest an indictment of contemporary America – a theme that recurs in Shepard's plays. Tourists abroad and in their own country, Kent and Salem suffer in Act 1 from the food and climate of Mexico, but they cannot be cured by that country's rituals, to which they feel superior. At home in the United States, however, suffering from sleeping sickness, Kent cannot be cured by an outworn popular model of his own country. In both acts the father–son doctors are rooted in their own cultural ground, which proves to be quicksand for a contemporary American.

Kent seems to be a professional tourist in *La Turista*, but *Melodrama Play* (1967), written a few weeks later, dramatises the artist as a young musician. As *La Turista* reflects cowboy and monster films, *Melodrama Play* reflects gangster films and the rock music scene of the

1960s. The stage is dominated by large eyeless photographs of Bob Dylan, king of rock, and Robert Goulet, king of crooners. Rock star Duke Durgens wears '*extra long hair, shades, jeans, boots, vest, etc.*', as do Duke's brother Drake, his friend Cisco, and four members of a rock band present throughout the play.

Having composed a hit song, Duke is coerced by his manager Floyd to compose another hit, as Shepard's Horse-Dreamer will be coerced in *Geography of a Horse-Dreamer* to name a winner, as his Rabbit Brown will be coerced to create a hit disaster movie in *Angel City*, but his composer Niles will flee coercion in *Suicide in B Flat*. Actually it was Drake who composed the hit song of *Melodrama Play*, which his brother Duke then recorded and sold to Floyd. Ordering his girlfriend Dana to cut his hair, Duke moves from the Dylan to the Goulet image, whereupon Floyd orders his strongman Peter to guard Duke, Drake, Dana and Cisco until a song hit is produced, no matter who composes it. While Peter plays cat-and-mouse with the true composer Drake, Duke on the radio sings the hit song: 'So prisoners, get up out a' your homemade beds.' One by one, Duke, Cisco and Dana rise from the floor and leave the stage, since this is a melodrama *play*. Yet the final image is not playful. As Peter raises his club against the composer Drake, there is a knock on the door. Commerce knocking outside, thug bludgeoning inside – that is the precarious, melodramatic position of the artist.

Of the three fantasies written in 1967, *Forensic and the Navigators* is fuzziest as to plot and character. It was, however, the occasion of Shepard's initial acquaintance with his first wife, O-Lan, who gave her name to her role. She changes in the play from someone enslaved to two revolutionaries into an object of desire for an exterminator of revolutionaries. In an ending that explodes from nowhere, the whole setting goes up in smoke. Perhaps Shepard himself sensed the play's weakness, since it was followed by a two-year silence.

By 1970 Shepard had been commissioned by Jules Irving to write a play for the Vivian Beaumont Theatre of New York's Lincoln Center. The result was *Operation Sidewinder*, whose intricate spectacular plot has been succinctly summarised by critic John Lahr:

> A six-foot sidewinder, which is really an escaped military computer; black, white, and Indian renegades plotting to capture Air Force planes by putting dope in a military reservoir; a Hopi snake dance whose ritual transforms the sidewinder computer from military property to religious icon.

Winding through this labyrinthine intrigue is a handsome young couple – an aimless hippy and a honey-haired *ingénue*. Lifted from the tale of Indian Geronimo is half-breed Mickey Free, who first rescues Honey from the sidewinder and then welcomes the young couple to the concluding Indian ceremony. The grand finale resembles a Disneyland version of New Comedy – boy gets girl against a phantasmagoria of costumed dances, billowing breezes and coloured lights.

Shepard also ends *Mad Dog Blues* (1971) on song and dance, but it is a revel *ex machina*. Apparently written in a drugged state, the 'two-act adventure show' manipulates nine characters dear to an undrugged Shepard. The cowboy figure, Waco Texas, is joined by a rock star, Kosmo; a drug addict, Yahoudi; and popular figures of fact and fiction. On a bare stage these characters travel far and wide, through ocean and desert, within an island and across a frontier, past one another though they are close enough to touch. Two friends – Kosmo the rock star, who 'leads with his cock' and Yahoudi the drug addict, who 'sucks in the printed word' – separately leave New York City. In Frisco Kosmo conjures up Mae West, and in a vision Yahoudi finds Marlene Dietrich. Kosmo then collects cowboy Waco Texas, while Yahoudi joins up with Captain Kidd of the legendary treasure. All characters go hunting for the treasure, and they tumble through swift adventures redolent of films. Marlene leaves Yahoudi for Paul Bunyan, lonely without his blue ox, Babe.

Act II opens on Yahoudi's threats to Captain Kidd, echoing *The Treasure of the Sierra Madre*. As fast as film cuts, characters journey around the stage's treasure island. Yahoudi shoots Captain Kidd and then himself, falling on the treasure, where Kosmo and Mae discover him. Soon Jesse James robs Kosmo of treasure and Mae. Kosmo implores his friend Yahoudi to return to life and help him manoeuvre the other characters. In vain. Each character is locked in his own myth, but they nevertheless '*keep searching for each other but never meet, even though at times THEY may pass right by each other*'. Only Jesse James and Mae West travel together, with bags full of treasure. On Paul Bunyan's ox, they stampede across the border into the United States. When the treasure turns out to be bottle-caps, Jesse James heads home for Missouri, to which Mae invites all the others, including a resurrected Yahoudi. The play closes on an improbable celebration – the last of Shepard's plays to do so.

Only a month after *Mad Dog Blues* Shepard dramatised blues again. *Cowboy Mouth*, written in collaboration with Patti Smith, and first enacted by Shepard and Smith, is inevitably read biographically, but the play's drive and intensity belie the rumour that the writers composed it on a typewriter pushed back and forth between them across a table. A woman, Cavale, has kidnapped Slim from his wife and child in order to fashion him into a rock messiah: 'You gotta be like a rock-and-roll Jesus with a cowboy mouth.' In her studio littered with symbolic debris (notably a dead crow) the couple alternately quarrel, play scenes, play music, reminisce, and order food which a scarlet-shelled Lobsterman delivers. Cavale fascinates Slim with her tales of French outlaw artists – Villon, Genet and Nerval, who walked through Paris with a lobster on a leash. The couple again send for the Lobsterman, who sheds his red carapace when they begin to sing. Looking like a rock messiah, the ex-Lobsterman is given a gun by departing Slim. As the silent Lobsterman spins its chambers, Cavale tells *him* about Nerval who had a pet lobster and hanged himself on her birthday, whence her name Cavale or 'escape'. Brilliantly theatrical, the play implicitly denies its title. A cowboy mouth or a lobster shell – neither one heralds a messiah.

Melodrama Play, Mad Dog Blues, Cowboy Mouth are stages of preparation for Shepard's most incisive portrait of an artist, *The Tooth of Crime*, written in England in 1972. The title comes from a sonnet by Mallarmé, read to Shepard by Patti Smith. The French line translates, 'A heart that the tooth of crime cannot wound'. Mallarmé's sonnet contrasts a vulnerable persona with his invulnerable partner in vice, and Shepard's play contrasts vulnerable Hoss with invulnerable Crow. Like classical tragedy, *The Tooth of Crime* begins close to its climax: Hoss needs a kill. He fondles an array of weapons displayed by Becky, his servant, mistress and tutor. Wiser than Shakespeare's Caesar who ignored the stars, Hoss consults his Star-Man and is advised against moving. Wiser than Shakespeare's Richard II, he seeks counsel from Galactic Jack, who reassures him, 'A shootin' star, baby, High flyin' and no jivin'.

You is off to number nine.' But Hoss is not reassured and is almost relieved when his fear takes human shape. Becky reports that a Gypsy has been 'sussed' – Shepard's polyvalent borrowing from Cockney slang. Hoss sounds out his chauffeur, Cheyenne, about cruising, but this faithful retainer is reluctant to violate the code. Lacking support, Hoss seeks an ally in the East but learns of his suicide. Distraught, Hoss sends for the Doc to give him an injection, but he is not tranquillised. Warned against cruising, Hoss nevertheless is somewhat soothed by Becky's cruising song. Hoss stalks and knifes a dummy, then recalls the camaraderie of his youth. Alone on stage, he engages in an imaginary dialogue with his father: 'They're all countin' on me. The bookies, the agents, the Keepers. I'm a fucking industry.' Hoss speaks his father's reply: 'You're just a man, Hoss. Just a man.' Having accepted that limitation, Hoss awaits Crow. Weary, enthroned under a huge shadow of Crow, Hoss absorbs Crow's song 'Poison' to close Act I.

Act II opens with Crow alone on stage, dressed in the hard rock style of the 1960s. As Shakespeare's Prince Hal tried on his father's crown, Crow sits in Hoss's throne-like chair. When Hoss arrives, Crow addresses him in clipped metaphors: 'Got the molar chomps. Eyes stitched. You can vision what's sittin'. Very razor to cop z's sussin' me to be on the far end of the spectrum.' From his royal isolation, Hoss asks Crow for news of the outside world, then orders him off the throne and summons a referee to judge their agon. In Round 1 Crow attacks Hoss with a capsule biography of a coward. Ref awards the round to Crow. In Round 2 Hoss accuses Crow of denying his musical origins in the blues of the Blacks, but Crow counters, 'I'm in a different time.' The Ref declares it a draw. In Round 3 Crow ridicules Hoss's outdated music, and the Ref calls it a technical knockout. An infuriated Hoss shoots the Ref, thereby becoming a gypsy outside law.

Hoss turns to Crow for instructions in survival. In a digression imitating the film *Alphaville*, Becky enacts a seduction of her youth, with Hoss perhaps the aggressor. Hoss himself cannot learn to talk, walk, and sing like a gypsy. Like classical heroes, he prefers death to dishonour:

> Now stand back and watch some true style. The mark of a lifetime. A true gesture that won't never cheat on itself 'cause it's the last of its kind. It can't be taught or copied or stolen or sold. It's mine. An original. It is my life and my death in one clean shot.

Hoss falls upon that shot, and Crow pays him homage: 'A genius mark.' Crow's reign begins, and his final song is a prayer for supremacy, like Hoss's plea to his advisers at the play's beginning.

Embracing earlier Shepard themes – swiftly changing modes of art, mechanisation of popular culture, the artist who dies mid-career, the messianic hope of rock music, even a hint of father–son relations – *Tooth* explores American culture. Through highly imaged, rhythmic monologues and through duelling dialogues, Hoss and Crow reveal themselves intimately, and through them we gain insight into a contemporary cacophony of big business, crime, sports, astrology, art.

Shepard again dramatises the artist in *Angel City* and *Suicide in B Flat* (1976). The *Angel City* artist is Rabbit Brown, shabbily dressed, travelling by buckboard, tied to magic bundles. He is invited to Angel City to invent a disaster that will create a movie triumph. The *Suicide* artist is jazz composer Niles, who is the titular suicide or victim of murder. By the end of *Angel City* Rabbit is fanged and long-nailed, oozing green slime; he has metamorphosed into the mogul who summoned him. The B flat musician has responded to pressure by repeating himself artistically; in order to escape to his own original music, he has to simulate his own death. At first invisible to musicians and detectives, he is finally apprehended and handcuffed.

In 1976, the year of these satiric fantasies, Shepard also turned to realism. He had already confessed in 1974, 'I'd like to try a whole different way of writing now, which is very stark and not so flashy and not full of a lot of mythic figures and everything, and try to scrape it down to the bone as much as possible.'

Hardly stark and still mythic, *Curse of the Starving Class* (1976), *Buried Child* (1978) and *True West* (1980) are realistic in setting, straightforward in plot, more or less coherent in character, and sport a grim humour. The plays have been called American Gothic, and they may also be Shepard's attempts at Greek tragedy. He himself speaks of them as a 'family trilogy'. The starving class is a Western family on an avocado farm with some cattle; the child is buried on a Mid-Western farm gone to seed. Both Western and Mid-Western families are cursed, even as the House of Atreus. In *Starving Class* the curse is literally Emma's first menstrual period, and the figurative family inheritance: 'We inherit [the curse] and pass it down, and then pass it down again. It goes on and on like that without us.' The very names announce a hereditary curse: father Weston and son Wesley, mother Ella and daughter Emma – names with a family resemblance. Although the family members claim not to belong to the starving class, they do, starving for identity and dignity. Every family member keeps opening and closing the refrigerator door. Only son Wesley understands the magnitude of the curse: 'So it means more than losing a house. It means losing a country.' At the end of the play, mother and son recite a parable of the cat and the eagle, clawing at one another high in the air: 'And they come crashing down to earth. Both of them come crashing down. Like one whole thing.' Greedy America has seized its own killer, a domestic animal driven berserk far from its natural environment.

Neither parable nor imaginative monologue relieves the lower depths of Mid-Western farm life in *Buried Child*. Grandfather Dodge is a sedentary cougher solaced only by television and whiskey. Grandmother Halie in Whistlerian black flirts with a clergyman to promote a statue for her dead son. More or less alive are her sons Tilden, an ex-football star and present half-wit, and Bradley, a sadistic cripple before whom the others cower. Home to the family bosom come grandson musician Vince and his California girlfriend. Tilden, having dug up carrots and corn from the backyard, ends the play carrying the decayed corpse of a buried child. Realistically, Dodge has murdered his wife's probably incestuous infant, but symbolically youth is buried by the American family – incestuous, sadistic, idiotic and moribund.

In *True West* Shepard resurrects the old romantic subject of two antagonistic brothers. Ivy League Austin and ne'er-do-well Lee compete in the composition of a movie scenario about the true West. With neither parable nor monologue, the play's first act rollicks in a comedy of cross-purposes. But the second act belabours the weary Western motif and slows the comic pace until it can scarcely be redeemed by the final image of the two brothers, poised in opposition.

While working on his family trilogy Shepard collaborated with the actor Joe Chaikin on two sets of monologues with music. Both *Tongues* (1978) and *Savage/Love* (1979) are polyphonic within the monologues. The one, in Mel Gussow's crisp summary, is 'dialogue buzzing like mosquitoes around his ears', and the other ranges over the tenderness, destructiveness and sheer absurdity of human love.

Those irreconcilable facets pound at one another in Shepard's fourth family play, *Fool for Love* (1983). Although Shepard believes that it 'is really more about a woman than any play I've ever written', either May or Eddie, or indeed their spectator father, is a candidate for the play's title. Lovers and half-siblings, they are bound with elastic steel. What we see on stage is their lives in little, for May strains to be free of Eddie, but she is snapped back again and again. Their passionate exchanges are punctuated by a percussion of slamming doors and bodies hurtling against the walls of the seedy motel setting. At the last Eddie leaves May with a promise to come 'right back', May leaves with her suitcase, and their father, pointing into space, exults at the picture of 'the woman of my dreams. . . . And she's mine. All mine. Forever.' Is love's possession possible only in dreams? Less susceptible of analysis than Shepard's other family plays, *Fool for Love* is an erotic tempest in a pressure-cooker. At one point Eddie says to May and her date, 'There's not a movie in this town that can match the story I'm gonna tell.' Unfortunately, that is true of the movie of *Fool for Love*, with Sam Shepard playing Eddie, and all passion dispersed.

It is to be hoped that no fool for film will attack *A Lie of the Mind* (1987), which is predicated on the physical chasm between two homes, always before our eyes. For the first six scenes, however, we are in phone booths, hospitals, motels, where Jake, thinking he has killed his wife Beth, flees from himself. By the end of Act I Jake is in his boyhood bed, being spoon-fed by his mother. In Acts II and III the scenes alternate between the home of Beth's parents in Montana and that of Jake's mother in California. Ron Mottram has pointed out that Shepard links the two homes by many phrases or stage directions. In each home is an invalid – guiltily sick Jake in the one and brain-damaged Beth in the other. Jake's brother Frankie becomes the third invalid when he is mistaken for a deer and shot by Beth's father, who grudgingly allows the young man to convalesce in his home.

In his most complex play Shepard dwells on two families, wandering homesteaders and rooted hunters (in Mel Gussow's description), where the men thrive by exploiting the women. Within those families are generational conflicts and sibling rivalries. The drama opens with a marital explosion so great that Beth is nearly killed, but during the course of the play we witness the stable marriage of Beth's parents, grounded in paternal responsibility and maternal tenderness. Beth herself – 'She's got male in her' – wishes to marry the gentle, almost womanly Frankie, and by the play's end a subdued Jake blesses their union. His mother and sister, free of their men, set their house aflame and depart for their roots in Ireland. Across the stage chasm, Beth's parents ritualistically fold the American flag while Jake leaves Frankie and Beth in an embrace. With the second sight of the mentally feeble, Beth's mother looks across the American continent and muses, 'Looks like a fire in the snow. How could that be?' In this rich drama, there is hope of a fire in the snow, or a blend of masculinity and femininity.

Famous through films, Shepard has suffered easy reduction by critics; one sees him obsessed by father–son conflicts, another by quests that end at home, a third by escape from American materialism into an interior life. It is not, however, theme but image and rhythm that render Shepard's plays memorable – some of them. Often starting with an image, he then casts characters around it, and only then conceives events: 'I'm taking notes in as much detail as possible on an event that's happening somewhere inside me.' It is this detail that magnetises audiences to these events. Every Shepard critic has described the hypnotic quality of his monologues, but more pertinent is the way Shepard has learned to subdue these tirades to the dramatic exigencies of the particular play. Collage, fantasy and the recent larger-than-life tragic realism – the best plays in each of these modes startle the eye, haunt the ear, tickle the funny-bone, and lie long in the mind.

Shepard has been hailed as the all-American playwright, as though there were a virtue in speaking for a chosen people. Like his ancestor O'Neill, however, Shepard in maturity is dramatising a tragic America, mired in sin. Like the Fitzgerald of *The Great Gatsby*, Shepard is at once seduced by and critical of American wealth and its artefacts. Like Thomas Wolfe, he realises that you can't go home again – to a pastoral civilisation. Like no other American playwright, Shepard enfolds figures of popular culture into more lasting patterns of myth – true West, rock stars, detectives, science fiction. It was by chance that this Westerner by temperament found himself in New York's East Village in the mid-1960s. 'It was incredible luck', he has said, 'to be around when something like Off-Off-Broadway was getting off the ground. But the 1960s were kinda awful. I don't even want to think about it.'